The Global Flood

A biblical and scientific look at the catastrophe that changed the earth

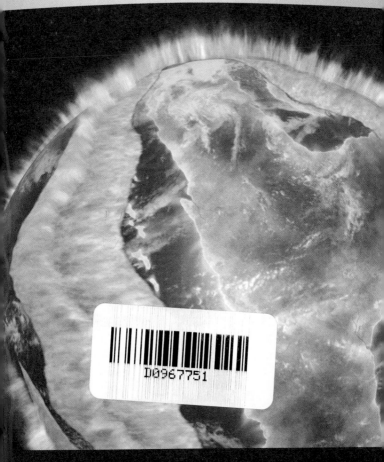

WAS THERE REALLY A WORLDWIDE FLOOD? • HIGH AND DRY SEA
CREATURES • TRANSCONTINENTAL ROCK LAYERS • RAPID EROSION
• FOLDED ROCK LAYERS • A CATASTROPHIC BREAKUP

A POCKET GUIDE TO . . .

The Global Flood

A biblical and scientific look at the catastrophe that changed the earth

Answers
IN GENESIS™

Petersburg, Kentucky, USA

Reprinted January 2016

ISBN: 978-1-60092-264-0

Printed in China

AnswersInGenesis.org

Table of Contents

Introduction

Should we be surprised that there are those—even those who profess to be Christians—who reject that the Flood was an actual, global event when Peter told that such a day would come? Looking to 2 Peter 3:5–6, we read:

> For this they willfully forget: that by the word of God the heavens were of old, and the earth standing out of water and in the water, by which the world that then existed perished, being flooded with water.

Reading the clearly described account in Genesis should leave no doubt in our minds that Moses intended to describe a deluge that covered the entire surface of the earth. In deceptive fashion, some will admit that the Flood was "universal," but really believe that it was a local flood that universally affected mankind.

We trust in a global Flood based on the revealed Word of God, however we should expect such an event to leave behind a multitude of evidence. When we look at the world around us—the layers of rock with billions of dead things buried in them—we must interpret the rocks according to our worldview. If, like the scoffers mentioned by Peter insist, we look at the world through the lens of millions of years we will come to the conclusion that a global Flood is impossible. If we submit ourselves to the authority and sufficiency of the Word of God, we can see the layers as the result of the Flood and interpret them properly. How have you interpreted the evidence in the rock layers? The following chapters present the evidence that supports the true and biblical account of the Flood.

Was There Really a Worldwide Flood?

by Ken Ham and Tim Lovett

The account of the Genesis Flood is one of the most widely known events in the history of mankind. Unfortunately, like other Bible accounts, it is often taken as a mere fairy tale.

The Bible, though, is the true history book of the universe, and in that light, the most-asked questions about the Flood of Noah's day can be answered with authority and confidence.

How could a flood destroy every living thing?

> And all flesh died that moved on the earth: birds and cattle and beasts and every creeping thing that creeps on the earth, and every man. All in whose nostrils was the breath of the spirit of life, all that was on the dry land, died (Genesis 7:21–22).

Noah's Flood was much more destructive than any 40-day rainstorm ever could be. Scripture says that the "fountains of the great deep" broke open. In other words, earthquakes, volcanoes, and geysers of molten lava and scalding water were squeezed out of the earth's crust in a violent, explosive upheaval. These fountains were not stopped until 150 days into the Flood—so the earth was literally churning underneath the waters for about five months! The duration of the Flood was extensive, and Noah and his family were aboard the Ark for over a year.

Relatively recent local floods, volcanoes, and earthquakes—though clearly devastating to life and land—are tiny in comparison to the worldwide catastrophe that destroyed "the world that then existed" (2 Peter 3:6). All land animals and people not on board the Ark were destroyed in the floodwaters—billions of animals were preserved in the great fossil record we see today.

How could the Ark survive the Flood?

The description of the Ark is very brief—Genesis 6:14–16. Those three verses contain critical information including overall dimensions, but Noah was almost certainly given more detail than this. Other divinely specified constructions in the Bible are meticulously detailed, like the descriptions of Moses's Tabernacle or the temple in Ezekiel's vision.

The Bible does not say the Ark was a rectangular box. In fact, Scripture gives no clue about the shape of Noah's Ark other than the proportions—length, width, and depth. Ships have long been described like this without ever implying a block-shaped hull.

Moses used the obscure term *tebah*, a word that is only used again for the basket that carried baby Moses (Exodus 2:3). One was a huge wooden ship and the other a tiny wicker basket. Both float, both rescue life, and both are covered. But the similarity ends there. We can be quite sure that the baby basket did not have the same proportions as the Ark, and Egyptian baskets of the time were typically rounded. Perhaps *tebah* means "lifeboat."

For many years biblical creationists have simply depicted the Ark as a rectangular box. This shape helped illustrate its size while avoiding the distractions of hull curvature. It also made it easy to compare volume. By using a short cubit and the maximum number of animal "kinds," creationists, as we've seen, have demonstrated how easily the Ark could fit the payload.[7] At the time, space was the main issue; other factors were secondary.

However, the next phase of research investigated sea-keeping (behavior and comfort at sea), hull strength, and stability. This began with a Korean study performed at the world-class ship research center (KRISO) in 1992.[8] The team of nine KRISO researchers was led by Dr. Hong, who is now director-general of the research center.

The study confirmed that the Ark could handle waves as high as 98 feet (30 m), and that the proportions of the biblical Ark are near optimal—an interesting admission from Dr. Hong, who believes evolutionary ideas, openly claiming "life came from the sea."[9] (For more details on the construction of the Ark, see *Pocket Guide to Noah's Ark*.)

Where did the floodwaters come from?

In telling us about the world-changing Flood in the days of Noah, the Bible gives us much information about where the waters came from and where they went. The sources of the water are given in Genesis 7:11 as "the fountains of the great deep" and the "windows of heaven."

The fountains of the great deep

The "fountains of the great deep" are mentioned before the "windows of heaven," indicating either relative importance or the order of events.

What are the "fountains of the great deep?" This phrase is used only in Genesis 7:11. "Fountains of the deep" is used in Genesis 8:2, where it clearly refers to the same thing, and Proverbs 8:28, where the precise meaning is not clear. "The great deep" is used three other times: Isaiah 51:10, where it clearly refers to the ocean; Amos 7:4, where God's fire of judgement is said to dry up the great deep, probably the oceans; and Psalm 36:6 where it is used metaphorically of the depth of God's justice/judgement. "The deep" is used more often, and usually refers to the oceans (e.g., Genesis 1:2; Job 38:30, 41:32; Psalm 42:7, 104:6; Isaiah 51:10, 63:13; Ezekiel 26:19; Jonah 2:3), but sometimes to subterranean sources of water (Ezekiel 31:4, 15). The Hebrew word (*mayan*) translated "fountains" means "fountain, spring, well."

So, the "fountains of the great deep" are probably oceanic or possibly subterranean sources of water. In the context of the Flood account, it could mean both.

If the fountains of the great deep were the major source of the waters, then they must have been a huge source of water. Some have suggested that when God made the dry land appear from under the waters on the third day of creation, some of the water that covered the earth became trapped underneath and within the dry land.[10]

Genesis 7:11 says that on the day the Flood began, there was a "breaking up" of the fountains, which implies a release of the water, possibly through large fissures in the ground or in the sea floor. The waters that had been held back burst forth with catastrophic consequences.

There are many volcanic rocks interspersed between the fossil layers in the rock record—layers that were obviously deposited during Noah's Flood. So it is quite plausible that these fountains of the great deep involved a series of volcanic eruptions with prodigious amounts of water bursting up through the ground. It is interesting that up to 70 percent or more of what comes out of volcanoes today is water, often in the form of steam.

In their catastrophic plate tectonics model for the Flood, Austin et al. have proposed that at the onset of the Flood, the ocean floor rapidly lifted by more than 3,500 feet (1,067 meters) due to the new warmer ocean crust being lighter as it formed from hot waters upwelling where the old, cold, dense ocean crust had broken up.[11] This would spill the seawater onto the land and cause massive flooding—perhaps what is aptly described as the breaking up of the "fountains of the great deep."

During the Flood, the world was deluged in 40 days of rain. But this was not the major source of the Flood waters.

The windows of heaven

The other source of the waters for Noah's Flood was "the windows of heaven." Genesis 7:12 says that it rained for 40 days and 40 nights continuously.

Genesis 2:5 tells us that there was no rain before man was created. Some have suggested that there was no rainfall anywhere on the earth until the time of the Flood. However, the Bible does not actually say this, so we should not be dogmatic.[12]

Some have argued that God's use of the rainbow as the sign of His covenant with Noah (Genesis 9:12-17) suggests that there were no rainbows, and therefore no clouds or rain, before the Flood. However, if rainbows (and clouds) existed before the Flood, this would not be the only time God used an existing thing as a special "new" sign of a covenant (e.g., bread and wine in the Lord's Supper).

It is difficult to envisage a pre-Flood water cycle without clouds and rain, as the sun's heat, even in that era, must have evaporated large volumes of surface waters which would have to eventually condense back into liquid water. And droplets of liquid water form clouds from which we get rain.

The expression "windows of heaven" is used twice in reference to the Flood (Genesis 7:11, 8:2). It is used only three times elsewhere in the Old Testament: twice in 2 Kings 7:2 and 19, referring to God's miraculous intervention in sending rain, and once in Malachi 3:10, where the phrase is used again of God intervening to pour out abundant blessings on his people. Clearly, in Genesis the expression suggests the extraordinary nature of the rainfall attending the Flood. It is not a term applied to ordinary rainfall.

Where did all the water go?

And the waters receded continually from the earth. At the end of the hundred and fifty days the waters decreased (Genesis 8:3).

Simply put, the water from the Flood is in the oceans and seas we see today. Three-quarters of the earth's surface is covered with water.

As even secular geologists observe, it does appear that the continents were at one time "together" and not separated by the vast oceans of today. The forces involved in the Flood were certainly sufficient to change all of this.

Scripture indicates that God formed the ocean basins, raising the land out of the water, so that the floodwaters returned to a safe place. (Some theologians believe Psalm 104 may refer to this event.) Some creation scientists believe this breakup of the continent was part of the mechanism that ultimately caused the Flood. (See "A Catastrophic Breakup," p. 75.)

Some have speculated, because of Genesis 10:25, that the continental break occurred during the time of Peleg. However, this division is mentioned in the context of the Tower of Babel's language division of the whole earth (Genesis 10–11). So the context points to a dividing of the languages and people groups, not the land breaking apart.

If there were a massive movement of continents during the time of Peleg, there would have been another worldwide flood. The Bible indicates that the mountains of Ararat existed for the Ark to land in them (Genesis 8:4); so the Indian-Australian Plate and Eurasian Plate had to have already collided, indicating that the continents had already shifted prior to Peleg.

Was Noah's Flood global?

And the waters prevailed exceedingly on the earth, and all the high hills under the whole heaven were covered. The waters prevailed fifteen cubits upward, and the mountains were covered (Genesis 7:19–20).

Many Christians today claim that the Flood of Noah's time was only a local flood. These people generally believe in a local flood because they have accepted the widely believed evolutionary history of the earth, which interprets fossil layers as the history of the sequential appearance of life over millions of years.[13]

Scientists once understood the fossils, which are buried in water-carried sediments of mud and sand, to be mostly the result of the great Flood. Those who now accept millions of years of gradual accumulation of fossils have, in their way of thinking, explained away the evidence for the global Flood. Hence, many compromising Christians insist on a local flood.

Secularists deny the possibility of a worldwide Flood at all. If they would think from a biblical perspective, however, they would see the abundant evidence for the global Flood. As someone once quipped, "I wouldn't have seen it if I hadn't believed it."

A local flood that rose above the mountains?

Those who accept the evolutionary time frame, with its fossil accumulation, also rob the Fall of Adam of its serious consequences. They put the fossils, which testify of disease, suffering, and death, before Adam and Eve sinned and brought death and suffering into the world. In doing this, they also undermine the meaning of the death and resurrection of Christ. Such a scenario also robs all meaning from God's description of His finished creation as "very good."

If the Flood only affected the area of Mesopotamia, as some claim, why did Noah have to build an Ark? He could have walked to the other side of the mountains and escaped. Most importantly, if the Flood were local, people not living in the vicinity of the Flood would not have been affected by it. They would have escaped God's judgment on sin.

In addition, Jesus believed that the Flood killed every person not on the Ark. What else could Christ mean when He likened the coming world judgment to the judgment of "all" men in the days of Noah (Matthew 24:37–39)?

In 2 Peter 3, the coming judgment by fire is likened to the former judgment by water in Noah's Flood. A partial judgment in Noah's day, therefore, would mean a partial judgment to come.

If the Flood were only local, how could the waters rise to 20 feet (6 m) above the mountains (Genesis 7:20)? Water seeks its own level; it could not rise to cover the local mountains while leaving the rest of the world untouched.

Even what is now Mt. Everest was once covered with water and uplifted afterward.[14] If we even out the ocean basins and flatten out the mountains, there is enough water to cover the entire earth by about 1.7 miles (2.7 km).[15] Also important to note is that, with the leveling out of the oceans and mountains, the Ark would not have been riding at the height of the current Mt. Everest, thus no need for such things as oxygen masks either.

There's more. If the Flood were a local flood, God would have repeatedly broken His promise never to send such a flood again. God put a rainbow in the sky as a covenant between God and man and the animals that He would never repeat such an event. There have been huge local floods in recent times (e.g., in Bangladesh); but never has there been another global Flood that killed all life on the land.

Where is the evidence in the earth for Noah's Flood?

> For this they willingly forget: that by the word of God the heavens were of old, and the earth standing out of water and in the water, by which the world that then existed perished, being flooded with water (2 Peter 3:5–6).

Evidence of Noah's Flood can be seen all over the earth, from seabeds to mountaintops. Whether you travel by car, train, or plane, the physical features of the earth's terrain clearly indicate a catastrophic past, from canyons and craters to coal beds and caverns. Some layers of strata extend across continents, revealing the effects of a huge catastrophe.

The earth's crust has massive amounts of layered sedimentary rock, sometimes miles (kilometers) deep! These layers of sand, soil, and material—mostly laid down by water—were once soft like mud, but they are now hard stone. Encased in these sedimentary layers are billions of dead things (fossils of plants and animals) buried very quickly. The evidence all over the earth is staring everyone in the face.

Where is Noah's Ark today?

> Then the Ark rested in the seventh month, the seventeenth day of the month, on the mountains of Ararat (Genesis 8:4).

The Ark landed in mountains. The ancient name for these mountains could refer to several areas in the Middle East, such as Mt. Ararat in Turkey or other mountain ranges in neighboring countries.

Mt. Ararat has attracted the most attention because it has permanent ice, and some people report having seen the Ark. Many expeditions have searched for the Ark there. There is no conclusive evidence of the Ark's location or survival; after all, it landed on the mountains about 4,500 years ago. Also it could easily have deteriorated, been destroyed, or been used as lumber by Noah and his descendants.

Some scientists and Bible scholars, though, believe the Ark could indeed be preserved—perhaps to be providentially revealed at a future time as a reminder of the past judgment and the judgment to come, although the same could be said for things like the Ark of the Covenant or other biblical icons. Jesus said, "If they do not hear Moses and the prophets, neither will they be persuaded though one rise from the dead" (Luke 16:31).

The Ark is unlikely to have survived without supernatural intervention, but this is neither promised nor expected from Scripture. However, it is a good idea to check if it still exists.

Why did God destroy the earth that He had made?

Then the Lord saw that the wickedness of man was great in the earth, and that every intent of the thoughts of his heart was only evil continually. But Noah found grace in the eyes of the Lord (Genesis 6:5, 8).

These verses speak for themselves. Every human being on the face of the earth had turned after the wickedness in their own hearts, but Noah, because of his righteousness before God, was spared from God's judgment, along with his wife, their sons, and their wives. As a result of man's wickedness, God sent judgment on all mankind. As harsh as the destruction was, no living person was without excuse.

God also used the Flood to separate and to purify those who believed in Him from those who didn't. Throughout history and throughout the Bible, this cycle has taken place time after time: separation, purification, judgment, and redemption.

Without God and without a true knowledge and understanding of Scripture, which provides the true history of the world, man is doomed to repeat the same mistakes over and over again.

How is Christ like the Ark?

For the Son of Man has come to save that which was lost (Matthew 18:11).

As God's Son, the Lord Jesus Christ is like Noah's Ark. Jesus came to seek and to save the lost. Just as Noah and his family were saved by the Ark, rescued by God from the floodwaters, so anyone who believes in Jesus as Lord and Savior will be spared from the coming final judgment of mankind, rescued by God from the fire that will destroy the earth after the last days (2 Peter 3:7).

Noah and his family had to go through a doorway into the Ark to be saved, and the Lord shut the door behind them (Genesis 7:16). So we too have to go through a "doorway" to be saved so that we won't be eternally separated from God. The Son of God, Jesus, stepped into history to pay the penalty for our sin of rebellion. Jesus said, "I am the door. If anyone enters by Me, he will be saved, and will go in and out and find pasture" (John 10:9).

---

1. The cubit was defined as the length of the forearm from elbow to fingertip. Ancient cubits vary anywhere from 17.5 inches (45 cm) to 22 inches (56 cm), the longer sizes dominating the major ancient constructions. Despite this, even a conservative 18 inch (46 cm) cubit describes a sizeable vessel.

2. For the evidence, see Donald Chittick, *The Puzzle of Ancient Man* (Newberg, OR: Creation Compass, 1998). This book details evidence of man's intelligence in early post-Flood civilizations.

---

3. For some remarkable evidence that dinosaurs have lived until relatively recent times, see chapter 12 of *The New Answers Book 1* (Green Forest, AR: New Leaf Press, 2006). Also read Ken Ham, *The Great Dinosaur Mystery Solved* (Green Forest, AR: New Leaf Press, 2000). Also visit www. answersingenesis.org/go/dinosaurs.

4. John Woodmorappe, *Noah's Ark: A Feasibility Study* (Santee, CA: Institute for Creation Research, 2003).

5. Here's one example: more than 200 different breeds of dogs exist today, from the miniature poodle to the St. Bernard—all of which have descended from one original dog "kind" (as have the wolf, dingo, etc.). Many other types of animals—cat kind, horse kind, cow kind, etc.—have similarly been naturally and selectively bred to achieve the wonderful variation in species that we have today. God "programmed" this variety into the genetic code of all animal kinds—even humankind! God also made it impossible for the basic "kinds" of animals to breed and reproduce with each other. For example, cats and dogs cannot breed to make a new type of creature. This is by God's design, and it is one fact that makes evolution impossible.

6. John Woodmorappe, *Noah's Ark: A Feasibility Study* (Santee, CA: Institute for Creation Research, 1996), p. 16.

7. Ibid.

8. Seok Won Hong et al., "Safety Investigation of Noah's Ark in a Seaway," *TJ* 8 no. 1 (1994): 26–36, www.answersingenesis.org/tj/v8/i1/noah.asp.

9. Seok Won Hong, "Warm greetings from the Director-General of MOERI (former KRISO), Director-General of MOERI/KORDI," http://www.moeri.re.kr/eng/about/about.htm.

10. Evidence is mounting that there is still a huge amount of water stored deep in the earth in crystal lattices of minerals, which is possible because of the immense pressure. See L. Bergeron, "Deep waters," *New Scientist*, 1997, 155(2097): 22-26:"You have oceans and oceans of water stored in the transition zone. It's sopping wet."

11. S.A. Austin, J.R. Baumgardner, D.R. Humphreys, A.A. Snelling, L. Vardiman, and K.P. Wise, "Catastrophic Plate Tectonics: A Global Flood Model of Earth History," in *Proceedings of the Third International Conference of Creationism*, ed. R.E. Walsh (Pittsburgh: Creation Science Fellowship, 1994), pp. 609-621.

12. Some have claimed that because the people scoffed at Noah's warnings of a coming flood, that they must not have seen rain. But people today have seen lots of rain and floods, and many still scoff at the global flood. Genesis 2:5 says there was no rain yet upon the earth, but whether or not it rained after that in the pre-flood world is not stated.

13. For compelling evidence that the earth is not billions of years old, read *The Young Earth* by Dr. John Morris and *Thousands . . . not Billions* by Dr. Don DeYoung; also see http://www. answersingenesis.org/young.

14. Mount Everest is more than 5 miles (8 km) high. How, then, could the Flood have covered "all the mountains under the whole heaven?" Before the Flood, the mountains were not so high. The mountains today were formed only towards the end of, and after, the Flood by collision of the tectonic plates and the associated up-thrusting. In support of this, the layers that form the uppermost parts of Mt. Everest are themselves composed of fossil-bearing, water-deposited layers.

15. A.R. Wallace, *Man's Place in the Universe* (New York: McClure, Phillips & Co, 1903), pp. 225–226; www.wku.edu/~smithch/wallace/S728-3.htm.

Ken Ham is President and CEO of Answers in Genesis–USA and the Creation Museum. Ken's bachelor's degree in applied science (with an emphasis on environmental biology) was awarded by the Queensland Institute of Technology in Australia. He also holds a diploma of education from the University of Queensland. In recognition of the contribution Ken has made to the church in the USA and internationally, Ken has been awarded two honorary doctorates: a Doctor of Divinity (1997) from Temple Baptist College in Cincinnati, Ohio and a Doctor of Literature (2004) from Liberty University in Lynchburg, Virginia.

Ken has authored or coauthored many books concerning the authority and accuracy of God's Word and the effects of evolutionary thinking, including *Genesis of a Legacy* and *The Lie: Evolution*.

Since moving to America in 1987, Ken has become one of the most in-demand Christian conference speakers and talk show guests in America. He has appeared on national shows such as Fox's *The O'Reilly Factor* and *Fox and Friends in the Morning*; CNN's *The Situation Room with Wolf Blitzer*, ABC's *Good Morning America*, the BBC, *CBS News Sunday Morning*, *The NBC Nightly News with Brian Williams*, and *The PBS News Hour with Jim Lehrer*.

Tim Lovett earned his degree in mechanical engineering from Sydney University (Australia) and was an instructor for 12 years in technical college engineering courses. Tim has studied the Flood and the Ark for 13 years and is widely recognized for his cutting-edge research on the design and structure of Noah's Ark.

Geologic Evidences for the Genesis Flood, Part 1:

An Overview

by Andrew A. Snelling

Have you ever been tongue-tied when asked to provide geologic evidence that the Genesis Flood really did occur, just as the Bible describes? Then what follows is for you.

This chapter provides an overview of six geologic evidences for the Genesis Flood, and in the series of six chapters to follow, each geologic evidence will be elaborated upon. Together, they will provide you with ammunition and a teaching tool for you and others.

Why is it that many people, including many Christians, can't see the geologic evidence for the Genesis Flood? It is usually because they have bought into the evolutionary idea that "the present is the key to the past." They are convinced that, because today's geological processes are so slow, the rock strata and the earth's rock layers took millions of years to form.

However, if the Genesis Flood really occurred, what evidence would we look for? We read in Genesis 7 and 8 that "the fountains of the great deep were broken up" and poured out water from inside the earth for 150 days (5 months). Plus it rained torrentially and globally for 40 days and nights ("the windows of heaven were opened"). No wonder all the high hills and the mountains were covered, meaning the earth was covered by a global ocean ("the world that then existed perished, being flooded with water," 2 Peter 3:6). All air-breathing life on the land was swept away and perished.

So what evidence would we look for? Wouldn't we expect to find billions of dead plants and animals buried and fossilized in sand, mud, and lime that were deposited rapidly by water in rock layers all over the earth? Of course! That's exactly what we find. Indeed, based on the description of the Flood in Genesis 7–8, there are six main geologic evidences that testify to the Genesis Flood.[1]

Six evidences for the Genesis Flood

Evidence #1—Fossils of sea creatures high above sea level due to the ocean waters having flooded over the continents.

We find fossils of sea creatures in rock layers that cover all the continents. For example, most of the rock layers in the walls of Grand Canyon (more than a mile above sea level) contain marine fossils. Fossilized shellfish are even found in the Himalayas.

Evidence #2—Rapid burial of plants and animals.

We find extensive fossil "graveyards" and exquisitely preserved fossils. For example, billions of nautiloid fossils are found in a layer within the Redwall Limestone of Grand Canyon. This layer was deposited catastrophically by a massive flow of sediment (mostly lime sand). The chalk and coal beds of Europe and the United States, and the fish, ichthyosaurs, insects, and other fossils all around the world, testify of catastrophic destruction and burial.

Evidence #3—Rapidly deposited sediment layers spread across vast areas.

We find rock layers that can be traced all the way across continents—even between continents—and physical features in those strata indicate they were deposited rapidly. For example, the Tapeats Sandstone and Redwall Limestone of Grand Canyon can be traced across the entire United States, up into Canada, and even across the Atlantic Ocean to England. The chalk beds of

England (the white cliffs of Dover) can be traced across Europe into the Middle East and are also found in the Midwest of the United States and in Western Australia. Inclined (sloping) layers within the Coconino Sandstone of Grand Canyon are testimony to 10,000 cubic miles of sand being deposited by huge water currents within days.

Evidence #4—Sediment transported long distances.

We find that the sediments in those widespread, rapidly deposited rock layers had to be eroded from distant sources and carried long distances by fast-moving water. For example, the sand for the Coconino Sandstone of Grand Canyon (Arizona) had to be eroded and transported from the northern portion of what is now the United States and Canada. Furthermore, water current indicators (such as ripple marks) preserved in rock layers show that for "300 million years" water currents were consistently flowing from northeast to southwest across all of North and South America, which, of course, is only possible over weeks during a global flood.

Evidence #5—Rapid or no erosion between strata.

We find evidence of rapid erosion, or even of no erosion, between rock layers. Flat, knife-edge boundaries between rock layers indicate continuous deposition of one layer after another, with no time for erosion. For example, there is no evidence of any "missing" millions of years (of erosion) in the flat boundary between two well-known layers of Grand Canyon—the Coconino Sandstone and the Hermit Formation. Another impressive example of flat boundaries at Grand Canyon is the Redwall Limestone and the strata beneath it.

Evidence #6—Many strata laid down in rapid succession.

Rocks do not normally bend; they break because they are hard and brittle. But in many places we find whole sequences of strata that were bent without fracturing, indicating that all the rock layers were rapidly deposited and folded while still wet and pliable before final hardening. For example, the Tapeats Sandstone in Grand Canyon is folded at a right angle (90°) without evidence of breaking. Yet this folding could only have occurred after the rest of the layers had been deposited, supposedly over "480 million years," while the Tapeats Sandstone remained wet and pliable.

Conclusion

Jesus Christ our Creator (John 1:1–3; Colossians 1:16–17), who is the Truth and would never tell us a lie, said that during the "days of Noah" (Matthew 24:37; Luke 17:26–27) "Noah entered the Ark" and "the Flood came and took them all away" (Matthew 24:38–39). He spoke of these events as real, literal history, describing a global Flood that destroyed all land life not on the Ark.

Therefore, we must believe what Christ told us, rather than the ideas of fallible scientists who weren't there to see what happened in the earth's past. Thus we shouldn't be surprised when the geologic evidence in God's world (rightly understood by asking the right questions) agrees exactly with God's Word, affirmed by Jesus Christ.

The next chapter will look in detail at the geologic evidence that the ocean waters flooded over the continents, just as described in Genesis 7–8.

---

1. I want to acknowledge that these geologic evidences have been elaborated on by my colleague Dr. Steve Austin at the Institute for Creation Research in his book *Grand Canyon: Monument to Catastrophe*, pages 51–52 (Institute for Creation Research, Santee, CA, 1994).

Dr. Andrew Snelling, one of the world's most respected creation scientists specializing in geological studies, joined Answers in Genesis in 2007.

Dr. Snelling completed a BS degree in Applied Geology at the University of New South Wales in Sydney, Australia, graduating with First Class Honors in 1975. He earned a PhD in geology from the University of Sydney. Dr. Snelling has worked as a consultant research geologist to organizations in both Australia and the U.S. Author of numerous scientific articles, Dr. Snelling is now the director of the Research Division at Answers in Genesis–USA.

Dr. Snelling is a member of many professional organizations, including the Geological Society of Australia, the Geological Society of America, and the Creation Research Society.

Geologic Evidences for the Genesis Flood, Part 2:

High and Dry Sea Creatures

by Andrew A. Snelling

If the Genesis Flood, as described in Genesis 7–8, really occurred, what evidence would we expect to find? The previous chapter gave an overview of the six main geologic evidences for the Genesis Flood. Now let's take a closer look at evidence number one.

After we read in Genesis 7 that all the high hills and the mountains were covered by water, and all air-breathing life on the land was swept away and perished, the answer to the question above should be obvious. Wouldn't we expect to find rock layers all over the earth that are filled with billions of dead animals and plants that were rapidly buried and fossilized in sand, mud, and lime? Of course, and that's exactly what we find.

Marine fossils high above sea level

It is beyond dispute among geologists that on every continent we find fossils of sea creatures in rock layers which today are high above sea level. For example, we find marine fossils in most of the rock layers in Grand Canyon. This includes the topmost layer in the sequence, the Kaibab Limestone exposed at the rim of the canyon, which today is approximately 7,000–8,000 feet (2,130–2,440 m) above sea level.[1] Though at the top of the sequence, this limestone must have been deposited beneath ocean waters loaded with lime sediment that swept over northern Arizona (and beyond).

Other rock layers exposed in Grand Canyon also contain large numbers of marine fossils. The best example is the Redwall Limestone, which commonly contains fossil brachiopods (a clam-like organism), corals, bryozoans (lace corals), crinoids (sea lilies), bivalves (types of clams), gastropods (marine snails), trilobites, cephalopods, and even fish teeth.[2]

These marine fossils are found haphazardly preserved in this limestone bed. The crinoids, for example, are found with their columnals (disks) totally separated from one another, while in life they are stacked on top of one another to make up their "stems." Thus, these marine creatures were catastrophically destroyed and buried in this lime sediment.

Marine fossils are also found high in the Himalayas, the world's tallest mountain range, reaching up to 29,029 feet (8,848 m) above sea level.[3] For example, fossil ammonites (coiled marine

Fossil ammonites (coiled marine cephalopods) like this one are found in limestone beds high in the Himalayas of Nepal. How did marine fossils get thousands of feet above sea level?

cephalopods) are found in limestone beds in the Himalayas of Nepal. All geologists agree that ocean waters must have buried these marine fossils in these limestone beds. So how did these marine limestone beds get high up in the Himalayas?

We must remember that the rock layers in the Himalayas and other mountain ranges around the globe were deposited during the Flood, well before these mountains were formed. In fact, many of these mountain ranges were pushed up by earth movements to their present high elevations at the end of the Flood. This is recorded in Psalm 104:8, where the Flood waters are described as eroding and retreating down valleys as the mountains rose at the end of the Flood.

The explanation

There is only one possible explanation for this phenomenon—the ocean waters at some time in the past flooded over the continents.

Could the continents have then sunk below today's sea level, so that the ocean waters flooded over them?

No! The continents are made up of lighter rocks that are less dense than the rocks on the ocean floor and rocks in the mantle beneath the continents. The continents, in fact, have an automatic tendency to rise, and thus "float" on the mantle rocks beneath, well above the ocean floor rocks.[4] This explains why the continents today have such high elevations compared to the deep ocean floor, and why the ocean basins can hold so much water.

So there must be another way to explain how the oceans covered the continents. The sea level had to rise, so that the ocean waters then flooded up onto—and over—the continents. What would have caused that to happen?

There had to be, in fact, two mechanisms.

First, if water were added to the ocean, then the sea level would rise.

The ocean floor rises

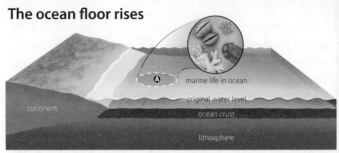

MARINE LIFE ORIGINALLY LIVES IN THE OCEAN Marine creatures obviously live in the ocean (**Ⓐ**). For these creatures to be deposited on the continents, the sea level had to rise.

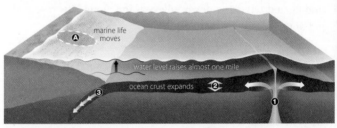

THE OCEAN CRUST IS HEATED AND EXPANDS **❶** During Noah's Flood molten rock was released from inside the earth and began replacing the original ocean crust. The ocean crust was effectively replaced by hot lavas. **❷** Because of the hot molten rock, the ocean crust became less dense and expanded. **❸** The molten rock displaced and pushed the original ocean crust below the continent. **Ⓐ** The sea level rose more than 3,500 feet (1,067 m) and marine creatures were carried onto the continent, buried in sediments, and fossilized.

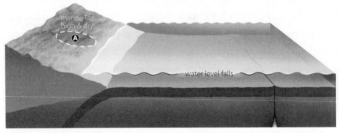

MARINE LIFE REMAINS ON THE CONTINENT Toward the end of the Flood, the ocean crust cooled and the ocean floor sank. As the waters drained off the continents, the sea level would have fallen, leaving marine fossils (**Ⓐ**) above sea level on the continents.

Scientists are currently monitoring the melting of the polar ice caps because the extra water would cause the sea level to rise and flood coastal communities.

The Bible suggests a source of the extra water. In Genesis 7:11 we read that at the initiation of the Flood all the fountains of the great deep were broken up. In other words, the earth's crust was split open all around the globe and water apparently burst forth as fountains from inside the earth. We then read in Genesis 7:24–8:2 that these fountains were open for 150 days. No wonder the ocean volume increased so much that the ocean waters flooded over the continents.

Second, if the ocean floor itself rose, it would then have effectively "pushed" up the sea level.

The Bible suggests a source of this rising sea floor: molten rock.

The catastrophic breakup of the earth's crust, referred to in Genesis 7:11, would not only have released huge volumes of water from inside the earth, but much molten rock.[5] The ocean floors would have been effectively replaced by hot lavas. Being less dense than the original ocean floors, these hot lavas would have had an expanded thickness, so the new ocean floors would have effectively risen, raising the sea level by more than 3,500 feet (1,067 m). Because today's mountains had not yet formed, and it is likely the pre-Flood hills and mountains were nowhere near as high as today's mountains, a sea level rise of over 3,500 feet would have been sufficient to inundate the pre-Flood continental land surfaces.

Toward the end of the Flood, when the molten rock cooled and the ocean floors sank, the sea level would have fallen and the waters would have drained off the continents into new, deeper ocean basins. As indicated earlier, Psalm 104:8 describes the mountains being raised at the end of the Flood and the Flood waters draining down valleys and off the emerging new land surfaces. This is consistent with much evidence that today's mountains only very recently rose to their present incredible heights.

Conclusion

The fossilized sea creatures and plants found in rock layers thousands of feet above sea level are thus silent testimonies to the ocean waters that flooded over the continents, carrying billions of sea creatures, which were then buried in the sediments these ocean waters deposited. This is how billions of dead marine creatures were buried in rock layers all over the earth.

We know that the cataclysmic Genesis Flood was an actual event in history because God tells us so in His record, the Bible. Now we can also see persuasive evidences that support what the Bible has so clearly taught all along.

1. R.L. Hopkins and K.L. Thompson, "Kaibab Formation," in *Grand Canyon Geology*, 2nd ed., eds. S.S. Beus and M. Morales (New York: Oxford University Press, 2003), pp. 196–211.

2. S.S. Beus, "Redwall Limestone and Surprise Canyon Formation," in *Grand Canyon Geology*, 2nd ed., eds. S.S. Beus and M. Morales (New York: Oxford University Press, 2003), pp. 115–135.

3. J.P. Davidson, W.E. Reed, and P.M. Davis, "The Rise and Fall of Mountain Ranges," in *Exploring Earth: An Introduction to Physical Geology* (Upper Saddle River, NJ: Prentice Hall, 1997), pp. 242–247.

4. J.P. Davidson, W.E. Reed, and P.M. Davis, "Isostasy," in *Exploring Earth: An Introduction to Physical Geology* (Upper Saddle River, NJ: Prentice Hall, 1997), pp. 124–129.

5. A.A. Snelling, "A Catastrophic Breakup: A Scientific Look at Catastrophic Plate Tectonics," *Answers* April–June 2007, pp. 44–48; A.A. Snelling, "Can Catastrophic Plate Tectonics Explain Flood Geology?" in K.A. Ham, ed., *The New Answers Book 1* (Green Forest, AR: Master Books, 2006), pp. 186–197.

Geologic Evidences for the Genesis Flood, Part 3:

The World's a Graveyard

by Andrew A. Snelling

*I*f the Genesis Flood, as described in Genesis 7 and 8, really occurred, what evidence would we expect to find? After noting in Genesis 7 that all the high hills and the mountains were covered by water and all air-breathing life on the land was swept away and perished, it should be obvious what evidence we would expect to find.

Wouldn't we expect to find rock layers all over the earth filled with billions of dead animals and plants that were buried rapidly and fossilized in sand, mud, and lime? Of course, and that's exactly what we find. Furthermore, even though the catastrophic geologic activity of the Flood would have waned in the immediate post-Flood period, ongoing mini-catastrophes would still have produced localized fossil deposits.

Graveyards around the world

Countless billions of plant and animal fossils are found in extensive "graveyards" where they had to be buried rapidly on a massive scale. Often the fine details of the creatures are exquisitely preserved.

For example, billions of straight-shelled, chambered nautiloids (Figure 1) are found fossilized with other marine creatures in a

FIGURE 1

FIGURE 2

7 foot (2 m) thick layer within the Redwall Limestone of Grand Canyon (Figure 2).[1] This fossil graveyard stretches for 180 miles (290 km) across northern Arizona and into southern Nevada, covering an area of at least 10,500 square miles (30,000 km²). These squid-like fossils are all different sizes, from small, young nautiloids to their bigger, older relatives.

To form such a vast fossil graveyard required 24 cubic miles (100 km³) of lime sand and silt, flowing in a thick, soup-like slurry at more than 16 feet (5 m) per second (more than 11 mph [18 km/h]) to catastrophically overwhelm and bury this huge, living population of nautiloids.

Hundreds of thousands of marine creatures were buried with amphibians, spiders, scorpions, millipedes, insects, and reptiles in a fossil graveyard at Montceau-les-Mines, France.[2] More than 100,000 fossil specimens, representing more than 400 species, have been recovered from a shale layer associated with coal beds in the Mazon Creek area near Chicago.[3] This spectacular fossil graveyard includes ferns, insects, scorpions, and tetrapods buried with jellyfish, mollusks, crustaceans, and fish, often with soft parts exquisitely preserved.

At Florissant, Colorado, a wide variety of insects, freshwater mollusks, fish, birds, and several hundred plant species (including nuts and blossoms) are buried together.[4] Bees and birds have to be buried rapidly in order to be so well preserved.

Alligator, fish (including sunfish, deep sea bass, chubs, pickerel, herring, and garpike 3–7 feet [1–2 m] long), birds, turtles, mammals, mollusks, crustaceans, many varieties of insects, and palm leaves (7–9 feet [2–2.5 m] long) were buried together in the vast Green River Formation of Wyoming.[5]

Notice in many of these examples how marine and land-dwelling creatures are found buried together. How could this have happened unless the ocean waters rose and swept over the continents in a global, catastrophic Flood?

FIGURE 3

FIGURE 4

FIGURE 5

At Fossil Bluff on the north coast of Australia's island state of Tasmania (Figure 3), many thousands of marine creatures (corals, bryozoans [lace corals], bivalves [clams], and gastropods [snails]) were buried together in a broken state, along with a toothed whale (Figure 4) and a marsupial possum (Figure 5).[6] Whales and possums don't live together, so only a watery catastrophe would have buried them together!

FIGURE 6

In order for such large ammonites (Figure 6) and other marine creatures to be buried in the chalk beds of Britain (Figure 7), many trillions of microscopic marine creatures (Figure 8) had to bury

FIGURE 7

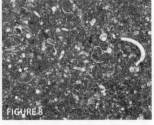

FIGURE 8

them catastrophically.[7] These same beds also stretch right across Europe to the Middle East, as well as into the Midwest of the USA, forming a global-scale fossil graveyard. In addition, more than 7 trillion tons of vegetation are buried in the world's coal beds found across every continent, including Antarctica.

Exquisite preservation

Such was the speed at which many creatures were buried and fossilized—under catastrophic flood conditions—that they were exquisitely preserved. Many fish were buried so rapidly, virtually alive, that even fine details of fins and eye sockets have been pre-

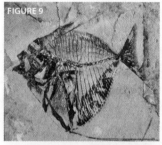
FIGURE 9

served (Figure 9). Many trilobites (Figure 10) have been so exquisitely preserved that even the compound lens systems in their eyes are still available for detailed study.

Mawsonites spriggi, when discovered, was identified as a fossilized jellyfish (Figure 11). It was found in a sandstone bed that covers more than 400 square miles (1,040 km²) of outback South Australia.[8] Millions of such soft-bodied marine creatures are exquisitely preserved in this sandstone bed.

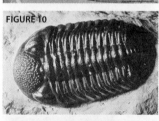
FIGURE 10

FIGURE 11

Consider what happens to soft-bodied creatures like jellyfish when washed up on a beach today. Because they consist only of soft "jelly," they

FIGURE 12

FIGURE 13

melt in the sun and are also destroyed by waves crashing onto the beach. Based on this reality, the discoverer of these exquisitely preserved soft-bodied marine creatures concluded that all of them had to be buried in less than a day!

Some fish were buried alive and fossilized so quickly in the geologic record that they were "caught in the act" of eating their last meal (Figure 12). Then there is the classic example of a female marine reptile, an ichthyosaur, about 6 feet (2 m) long, found fossilized at the moment of giving birth to her baby (Figure 13)! One minute this huge creature was giving birth, then seconds later, without time to escape, mother and baby were buried and "snap frozen" in a catastrophic "avalanche" of lime mud.

Conclusions

These are but a few examples of the many hundreds of fossil graveyards found all over the globe that are now well-documented in the geological literature.[9] The countless billions and billions of fossils in these graveyards, in many cases exquisitely preserved, testify to the rapid burial of once-living plants and animals on a global scale in a watery cataclysm and its immediate aftermath. Often these fossil graveyards consist of mixtures of marine and land-dwelling creatures, indicating that the waters of this global cataclysm swept over both the oceans and the continents.

When we again read the biblical account of the Flood and ask ourselves what evidence we should expect, the answer is obvious—billions of dead plants and animals buried in rock layers laid down by water all over the world. And that's exactly what we find. The global, cataclysmic Genesis Flood and its aftermath was an actual event in history, just as God tells us in His record of earth's history.

1.   Steven Austin, "Nautiloid Mass Kill and Burial Event, Redwall Limestone (Lower Mississippian), Grand Canyon Region, Arizona and Nevada," in *Proceedings of the Fifth International Conference on Creationism*, ed. R. L. Ivey (Pittsburgh: Creation Science Fellowship, 2003), pp. 55–99.

2.   Daniel Heyler and Cecile M. Poplin, "The Fossils of Montceau-les-Mines," *Scientific American*, September 1988, pp. 70–76.

3.   Charles Shabika and Andrew Hay, eds. *Richardson's Guide to the Fossil Fauna of Mazon Creek* (Chicago: Northeastern Illinois University, 1997).

4.   Theodore Cockerell, "The Fossil Flora and Fauna of the Florissant Shales," *University of Colorado Studies* 3 (1906): 157–176; Theodore Cockerell, "The Fossil Flora of Florissant, Colorado," *Bulletin of the American Museum of Natural History*, 24 (1908): 71–110.

5.   Lance Grande, "Paleontology of the Green River Formation with a Review of the Fish Fauna," *The Geological Survey of Wyoming Bulletin* 63 (1984).

6.   Andrew Snelling, "Tasmania's Fossil Bluff," *Ex Nihilo*, March 1985, pp. 6–10.

7.   Jake Hancock, "The Petrology of the Chalk," *Proceedings of the Geologists' Association* 86 (1975): 499–536; Andrew Smith and David Batten, "Fossils of the Chalk," *Field Guides to Fossils*, no. 2, 2nd ed. (London: The Palaeontological Association, 2002).

8.   Reginald Sprigg, "Early Cambrian (?) Jellyfishes from the Flinders Ranges, South Australia," *Transactions of the Royal Society of South Australia* 71, no. 2 (1947): 212–224; M. F. Glaessner and M. Wade, "The Late Precambrian Fossils from Ediacara, South Australia," *Palaeontology* 9 (1966): 599–628.

9.   For example: David Bottjer, Walter Etter, James Hagadorn, and Carol Tang, eds., *Exceptional Fossil Preservation: A Unique View on the Evolution of Marine Life* (New York: Columbia University Press, 2002).

Geologic Evidences for the Genesis Flood, Part 4:

Transcontinental Rock Layers

by Andrew A. Snelling

*W*hat evidence do we have that the Genesis Flood, as described in Genesis 7–8, really occurred? Genesis 7 explains that water covered all the high hills and the mountains, and that all air-breathing life on the land was swept away and perished. As part of the evidence of the Flood, we would expect to find rock layers all over the earth filled with billions of dead animals and plants that were rapidly buried and fossilized in sand, mud, and lime. And that's exactly what we find.

Rapidly deposited sediment layers spread across vast areas

On every continent are found layers of sedimentary rocks over vast areas. Many of these sediment layers can be traced all the way across continents, and even between continents. Furthermore, when geologists look closely at these rocks, they find evidence that the sediments were deposited rapidly.

Consider the sedimentary rock layers exposed in the walls of Grand Canyon in northern Arizona (Figure 1). This sequence of layers is not unique to that region of the USA. For more than 50 years

FIGURE 1

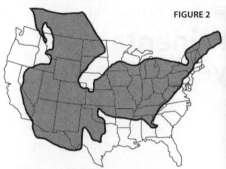

FIGURE 2

FIGURE 3

FIGURE 4

The sedimentary rock layers exposed in the walls of Grand Canyon (Figure 1) belong to six megasequences that can be traced across North America (Figure 2). At the base of these layers are huge boulders (Figure 3) and sand beds (Figure 4) that are evidences of sediments being laid down rapidly across the entire USA.

geologists have recognized that these strata belong to six megasequences (very thick, distinctive sequences of sedimentary rock layers) that can be traced right across North America.[1]

The lowermost sedimentary layers in Grand Canyon are the Tapeats Sandstone, belonging to the Sauk Megasequence. It and its equivalents (those layers comprised of the same materials) cover much of the USA (Figure 2). We can hardly imagine what forces were necessary to deposit such a vast, continent-wide series of deposits. Yet at the base of this sequence are huge boulders (Figure 3) and sand beds deposited by storms (Figure 4). Both are evidence that massive forces deposited these sediment layers rapidly and violently right across the entire USA. Slow-and-gradual (present-day uniformitarian) processes cannot account for this evidence, but the global catastrophic Genesis Flood surely can.

Another layer in Grand Canyon is the Lower Carboniferous (Mississippian) Redwall Limestone. This belongs to the Kaskaskia

Megasequence of North America. So the same limestones appear in many places across North America, as far as Tennessee and Pennsylvania. These limestones also appear in the exact same position in the strata sequences, and they have the exact same fossils and other features in them.

Unfortunately, these limestones have been given different names in other locations because the geologists saw only what they were working on locally and didn't realize that other geologists were studying essentially the same limestone beds in other places. Even more remarkable, the same Carboniferous limestone beds also appear thousands of miles east in England, containing the same fossils and other features.

Chalk beds

FIGURE 5

The chalk beds of southern England (above) can be traced across France, Germany, and Poland, all the way to the Middle East.

The Cretaceous chalk beds of southern England are well known because they appear as spectacular white cliffs along the coast (Figure 5). These chalk beds can be traced westward across England and appear again in Northern Ireland. In the opposite direction, these same chalk beds can be traced across France, the Netherlands, Germany, Poland, southern Scandinavia, and other parts of Europe to Turkey, then to Israel and Egypt in the Middle East, and even as far as Kazakhstan.[2]

Remarkably, the same chalk beds with the same fossils and the same distinctive strata above and below them are also found in the Midwest USA, from Nebraska in the north to Texas in the south. They also appear in the Perth Basin of Western Australia.

Coal beds

Consider another feature—coal beds. In the northern hemisphere, the Upper Carboniferous (Pennsylvanian) coal beds of the eastern and Midwest USA are the same coal beds, with the same plant fossils, as those in Britain and Europe. They stretch halfway around the globe, from Texas to the Donetz Basin north of the Caspian Sea in the former USSR.[3] In the southern hemisphere, the same Permian coal beds are found in Australia, Antarctica, India, South Africa, and even South America! These beds share the same kind of plant fossils across the region (but they are different from those in the Pennsylvanian coal beds).

Evidence of rapid deposition

Sloped beds of sandstone

The buff-colored Coconino Sandstone is very distinctive in the walls of Grand Canyon. It has an average thickness of 315 feet (96 m) and covers an area of at least 200,000 square miles (518,000 km²) eastward across adjoining states.[4] So the volume of sand in the Coconino Sandstone layer is at least 10,000 cubic miles (41,700 km³).

This layer also contains physical features called cross beds.

FIGURE 6

The Coconino Sandstone layer in Grand Canyon contains sloped layers of sandstone called cross beds. These beds are remnants of the sand waves produced by water currents during the Flood.

While the overall layer of sandstone is horizontal, these cross beds are clearly visible as sloped beds (Figure 6). These beds are remnants of the sand waves produced by the water currents that deposited the sand (like sand dunes, but underwater) (Figure 7). So it can be demonstrated that water, flowing at 3–5 miles per hour (4.8–8

FIGURE 7

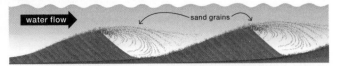

Strong, fast-flowing water currents move sands across the ocean floor as sand waves or dunes (above). As the sand grains are swept over the dune crests, they fall on the advancing dune faces to produce sloping sand beds, and on top of the trailing edges of the dunes in front. The dunes thus advance over one another, resulting in stacked sand layers (below) with internal sloping beds (cross beds).

km/h), deposited the Coconino Sandstone as massive sheets of sand, with sand waves up to 60 feet (18 m) high.[5] At this rate, the whole Coconino Sandstone layer (all 10,000 cubic miles of sand) would have been deposited in just a few days!

Distinctive and jagged minerals within sandstone

Ayers Rock (or Uluru) in central Australia consists of coarse-grained sandstone beds that are almost vertical, tilted at about 80° (Figure 8). The total thickness of these sandstone beds, outcropping in Ayers Rock and found under the surrounding desert sands, is 18,000–20,000 feet (5,500–6,100 m).[6] The minerals in the sand grains are distinctive, and the closest source of them is at least 63 miles (101 km) away.

FIGURE 8

FIGURE 9

Under the microscope the sand grains appear jagged and are of different sizes (Figure 9). One of the minerals is called feldspar, and it appears to be still unusually fresh in the sandstone. These features imply rapid transport and deposition of all this sand, before the feldspar grains could disintegrate or the sand grains could be worn down into round pebbles or sorted by size.[7]

So soup-like slurries of sediment, known as turbidity currents, which travel at speeds of up to 70 miles per hour (113 km/h), must have transported all this sand, 18,000–20,000 feet thick, a distance of at least 63 miles and deposited it as the Uluru Sandstone beds in a matter of hours! This defies evolution ideology but fits with the Creation/Flood history of Genesis.

God's judgment "clearly seen"

Sediment layers that spread across vast continents are evidence that water covered the continents in the past. Even more dramatic are the fossil-bearing sediment layers that were deposited rapidly right across many or most of the continents at the same time. To catastrophically deposit such extensive sediment layers implies global flooding of the continents. This brief chapter describes just a few of the many examples of rapidly deposited sediment layers spread across vast areas.[8]

As Noah's Flood catastrophically swept over all the continents to form a global ocean (described in Genesis 7–8), we would expect the waters to deposit fossil-bearing sediment layers rapidly across vast areas around the globe. And that is exactly what we find—further evidence that the global cataclysmic Genesis Flood was an actual event in history, just as God has told us in His eyewitness account of earth's history.

1. L.L. Sloss, "Sequences in the Cratonic Interior of North America," *Geological Society of America Bulletin* no. 74 (1963): 93–114.

2. D.V. Ager, *The Nature of the Stratigraphical Record* (London: Macmillan, 1973), pp. 1–2.

3. Ibid., pp. 6–7.

4. D.L. Baars, "Permian System of Colorado Plateau," *American Association of Petroleum Geologists Bulletin* no. 46 (1962): 200–201; J. M. Hills and F. E. Kottlowski, *Correlation of Stratigraphic Units of North America-Southwest/Southwest Mid-Continent Region, American Association of Petroleum Geologists* (Tulsa, Oklahoma, 1983); R. C. Blakey and R. Knepp, "Pennsylvanian and Permian Geology of Arizona," in J. P. Jenney, and S. J. Reynolds, eds., *Geologic Evolution of Arizona: Arizona Geological Society Digest*, vol. 17 (1989): 313–347.

5. A.A. Snelling and S.A. Austin, "Startling Evidence of Noah's Flood," *Creation Ex Nihilo* 15, no. 1 (1992): 46–50; S.A. Austin, ed., *Grand Canyon: Monument to Catastrophe* (Santee, CA: Institute for Creation Research, 1994), pp. 28–36.

6. C.R. Twidale, "On the Origin of Ayers Rock, Central Australia," *Zeitschrift für Geomorphologie Neue Folge Supplement* no. 31 (1978): 177–206; J. Selby, "Ayers Rock," *Geology Today* 5, no.6 (1989): 206–209; I. P. Sweet and I. H. Crick, *Uluru and Kata Tjuta* (Canberra: Australian Geological Survey Organisation, 1992).

7. A.A. Snelling, "The Origin of Ayers Rock," *Ex Nihilo* 7, no. 1 (1984): 6–9; A. A. Snelling, "Uluru and Kata Tjuta: Testimony to the Flood," *Creation* 20, no. 2 (1998): 36–40.

8. D.V. Ager, *The Nature of the Stratigraphical Record* (London: Macmillan, 1973), pp. 1–13.

Geologic Evidences for the Genesis Flood, Part 5:

Sand Transported Cross Country

by Andrew A. Snelling

*I*n previous chapters we have already seen the evidence that rapidly deposited sediment layers containing rapidly buried plant and animal fossils are found spread across vast areas, often high above sea level. No known slow-and-gradual geologic processes in the present world are currently producing such fossiliferous sediment layers spread across continents. Though evolutionary geologists are loath to admit it, only a global flood in which the ocean waters flooded over the continents could have done this.

Sediment transported long distances

Now it logically follows that, when the Flood waters swept over the continents and rapidly deposited sediment layers across vast areas, these sediments had to have been transported long distances. In other words, the sediments in the strata had to come from distant sources. And that's exactly the evidence we find.

For example, in the previous chapter we discussed the Coconino Sandstone, seen spectacularly in the walls of Grand Canyon (Figure 1). It has an average thickness of 315 feet (96 m), covers an area of at least 200,000 square miles (518,000 km²),

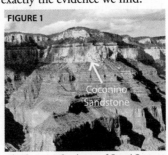

FIGURE 1

The Coconino Sandstone of Grand Canyon

and thus contains at least 10,000 cubic miles (41,700 km³) of sand.[1] Where did this sand come from, and how do we know?

The sand grains are pure quartz (a natural glass mineral), which is why the Coconino Sandstone is such a distinctive buff color. Directly underneath it is the strikingly different red-brown Hermit Formation, consisting of siltstone and shale. Sand for the Coconino Sandstone could not have come from the underlying Hermit Formation.

The sloping remnants of sand "waves" in the Coconino Sandstone point to the south, indicating the water that deposited the sand flowed from the north.[2] Another clue is that the Coconino Sandstone thins to zero to the north in Utah, but the Hermit Formation spreads farther into Utah and beyond. So the Coconino's pure quartz sand had to come from a source even farther north, above and beyond the red-brown Hermit.

Grand Canyon has another set of layers with sand that must have come from far away—the sandstone beds within the Supai Group strata between the Hermit Formation and the Redwall Limestone. In this case, the sand "wave" remnants point to the southeast, so the sand grains had to have been deposited by water flowing from a source in the north and west. However, to the north and west of Grand Canyon we find only Redwall Limestone underneath the Supai Group, so there is no nearby source of quartz sand for these sandstone beds.[3] Thus an incredibly long distance must be postulated for the source of Supai Group sand grains.[4]

Other sediment even transported across the continent

A third layer of sandstone higher in the strata sequence gives us a clue. The Navajo Sandstone of southern Utah, best seen in the spectacular mesas and cliffs in and around Zion National Park (Figure 2), is well above the Kaibab Limestone, which forms the rim

FIGURE 2

The Navajo Sandstone of southern Utah

rock of Grand Canyon. Like the Grand Canyon sandstones, this sandstone also consists of very pure quartz sand, giving it a distinctly brilliant white color, and it also contains remnants of sand "waves."

Within this sandstone, we find grains of the mineral zircon, which is relatively easy to trace to its source because zircon usually contains radioactive uranium. By "dating" these zircon grains, using the uranium-lead (U-Pb) radioactive method, it has been postulated that the sand grains in the Navajo Sandstone came from the Appalachians of Pennsylvania and New York, and from former mountains further north in Canada. If this is true, the sand grains were transported about 1,250 miles (2012 km) right across North America (Figure 3).[5]

This "discovery" poses somewhat of a dilemma for conventional uniformitarian (slow-and-gradual) geologists, because no known sediment transport system is capable of carrying sand across the entire North American continent during the required millions of years. It must have been water over an area even bigger than the continent. All they can do is postulate that some unknown transcontinental river system must have done the job. But even in their scientific belief system of earth history, it is impossible for such a river to have persisted for millions of years.

Yet the evidence is overwhelming that the water was flowing in one direction. More than half a million measurements have been collected from 15,615 North American localities, recording water current direction indicators throughout the geologic record. The evidence indicates that water moved sediments across the entire continent, from the east and northeast to the west and southwest throughout the so-called Paleozoic.[6] This general

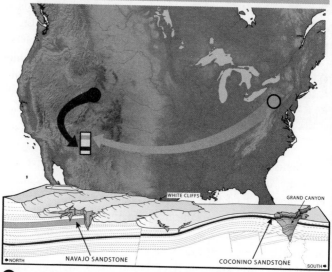

WHITE CLIFFS

GRAND CANYON

NORTH

NAVAJO SANDSTONE

COCONINO SANDSTONE

SOUTH

The distinctive sand grains found in the Coconino Sandstone of Grand Canyon are pure quartz and were most likely transported from a source as far as northern Utah or Wyoming.

In southern Utah, the Navajo Sandstone is made of distinctive sand grains that were most likely transported from the Appalachians of Pennsylvania and New York.

pattern continued on up into the Mesozoic, when the Navajo Sandstone was deposited. How could water be flowing across the North American continent consistently for hundreds of millions of years? Absolutely impossible!

The only logical and viable explanation is the global cataclysmic Genesis Flood. Only the water currents of a global ocean, lasting a few months, could have transported such huge volumes of sediments right across the North American continent to deposit the thick strata sequences which blanket the continent.[7]

The geologic record has many examples of sediments that did not come from erosion of local, underlying rocks. Rather, the sediments had to have been transported long distances, in some cases even across continents. This is confirmed by water current direction indicators in these sedimentary layers, which show a consistent uni-directional flow. However, conjectured transcontinental river systems could not have operated like that for hundreds of millions of years. Instead, only catastrophic global flooding of the continents over a few months can explain the huge volumes of sediments transported across the continents.

In Genesis 7–8 the Bible describes the cataclysmic global Flood in which the waters covered the whole earth, sweeping across entire continents. We would expect to find that these global waters eroded sediments and transported them across whole continents to be deposited in layers covering vast areas. We have now seen that this is exactly what we find across North America, so there is no excuse for claiming there is no evidence of a global flood. The global cataclysmic Genesis Flood actually happened in the earth's history, just as God told us it did.

1.   D.L. Baars, "Permian System of Colorado Plateau," *American Association of Petroleum Geologists Bulletin* 46 (1962): 200–201; J.M. Hills and F.E. Kottlowski, *Correlation of Stratigraphic Units of North America-Southwest/Southwest Mid-Continent Region* (Tulsa, Oklahoma: American Association of Petroleum Geologists, 1983); R.C. Blakey and R. Knepp, "Pennsylvanian and Permian Geology of Arizona," in J.P. Jenney and S.J. Reynolds, eds., "Geologic Evolution of Arizona," *Arizona Geological Society Digest* 17 (1989): 313–347.

2.   S.A. Austin, ed. *Grand Canyon: Monument to Catastrophe*, (El Cajon, CA: Institute for Creation Research, 1994), p. 36.

3.   J.S. Shelton, *Geology Illustrated* (San Francisco: W.H. Freeman, 1966), p. 280.

4.   R.C. Blakey, "Stratigraphy of the Supai Group (Pennsylvanian-Permian), Mogollon Rim, Arizona," in S.S. Beus and R.R. Rawson, eds., *Carboniferous Stratigraphy in the Grand Canyon Country, Northern Arizona and Southern Nevada* (Falls Church, VA: American Geological Institute, 1979), p. 102.

5.   J.M. Rahl, P.W. Reiners, I.H. Campbell, S. Nicolescu, and C.M. Allen, "Combined Single-Grain (U-Th)/He and U/Pb Dating of Detrital Zircons from the Navajo Sandstone, Utah," *Geology* 31.9 (2003): 761–764; S.R. Dickinson and G.E. Gehrels, "U-Pb Ages of Detrital Zircons from Permian and Jurassic Eolian Sandstones of the Colorado Plateau, USA: Paleogeographic Implications," *Sedimentary Geology* 163 (2003): 29–66.

6.   A.V. Chadwick, "Megatrends in North American Paleo-currents," http://origins.swau.edu/papers/global/paleocurrents/default.html, 2007.

7.   L.L. Sloss, "Sequences in the Cratonic Interior of North America," *Geological Society of America Bulletin* 74 (1963): 93–114.

Geologic Evidences for the Genesis Flood, Part 6:

No Slow and Gradual Erosion

by Andrew A. Snelling

*I*n this chapter we'll look more closely at a feature that is often overlooked—the boundaries between rock layers. What should they look like, if laid down during a single, global Flood?

Today we see the effects of weathering and erosion all around us. But where is the evidence of millions of years between rock layers? There is none.

The dominant view today is that slow and gradual (uniformitarian) processes, similar to the processes we observe in the present, explain the thick, fossil-bearing sedimentary rock layers all over the earth. These slow geologic processes would require hundreds of millions of years to deposit all the successive sediment layers. Furthermore, this popular view holds that slow weathering and erosion gradually wore away the earth's surface to produce its relief features, such as hills and valleys.

This view has a problem, however. If the fossil-bearing layers took hundreds of millions of years to accumulate, then we would expect to find many examples of weathering and erosion after successive layers were deposited. The boundaries between many sedimentary strata should be broken by lots of topographic relief with weathered surfaces. After all, shouldn't millions of years worth of weathering and erosion follow each deposition?

On the other hand, the cataclysmic global Flood described in Genesis 7–8 would lead us to expect something much different.

Most of the fossil-bearing layers would have accumulated in just over one year. Under such catastrophic conditions, even if land surfaces were briefly exposed to erosion, such erosion (called sheet erosion) would have been rapid and widespread, leaving behind flat and smooth surfaces. The erosion would not create the localized topographic relief (hills and valleys) we see forming at today's snail's pace. So, if the Genesis Flood caused the fossil-bearing geologic record, then we would only expect evidence of rapid or no erosion at the boundaries between sedimentary strata.

So what evidence do we find? At the boundaries between some sedimentary layers we find evidence of only rapid erosion. In most other cases, the boundaries are flat, featureless, and knife-edged, with absolutely no evidence of any erosion, which is consistent with no long periods of elapsed time, as would be expected during the global, cataclysmic Genesis Flood.

Examples in Grand Canyon

Grand Canyon in the southwestern United States offers numerous examples of strata boundaries that are consistent with deposition during the Genesis Flood.[1] However, we will focus here on just four, which are typical of all the others. These boundaries

FIGURE 1

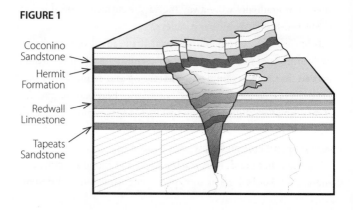

Coconino Sandstone

Hermit Formation

Redwall Limestone

Tapeats Sandstone

appear at the bases of the Tapeats Sandstone, Redwall Limestone, Hermit Formation, and Coconino Sandstone

Below Tapeats Sandstone

The strata below the Tapeats Sandstone has been rapidly eroded and then extensively scraped flat (planed off). We know that this erosion occurred on a large scale because we see its effects from one end of Grand Canyon to the other. This massive erosion affected many different underlying rock layers—granites and metamorphic rocks, and tilted sedimentary strata.

There are two evidences that this large-scale erosion was rapid. First, we don't see any evidence of weathering below the boundary[2] (Figure 2). If there were weathering, we would expect to see soils, but we don't. Second, we find boulders and features known as "storm beds" in the Tapeats Sandstone above the boundary[3] (Figure 3). Storm beds are sheets of sand with unique internal features produced only by storms, such as hurricanes. Boulders and storm beds aren't deposited slowly.

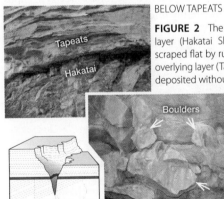

BELOW TAPEATS SANDSTONE

FIGURE 2 The surface of the lower layer (Hakatai Shale) was completely scraped flat by rushing water. Then the overlying layer (Tapeats Sandstone) was deposited without further erosion.

FIGURE 3 Fast-moving water currents would explain the movement of boulders like these deposited in the base of the Tapeats Sandstone.

Below Redwall Limestone

Below the base of the Redwall Limestone the underlying Muav Limestone has been rapidly eroded in a few localized places to form channels (Figure 4). These channels were later filled with lime sand to form the Temple Butte Limestone. Apart from these rare exceptions, the boundary between the Muav and Redwall Limestones, as well as the boundary between the Temple Butte and Redwall Limestones, are flat and featureless, hallmarks of continuous deposition.

Indeed, in some locations the boundary between the Muav and Redwall Limestones is impossible to find because the Muav Limestone continued to be deposited after the Redwall Limestone began.[4] This feature presents profound problems for uniformitarian geology. The Muav Limestone was supposedly deposited 500–520 million years ago,[5] the Temple Butte Limestone was supposedly deposited about 100 million years later (350–400 million years ago),[6] and then the Redwall Limestone deposited several million years later (330–340 million years ago).[7] Based on the evidence, it is much more logical to believe that these limestones were deposited continuously, without any intervening millions of years.

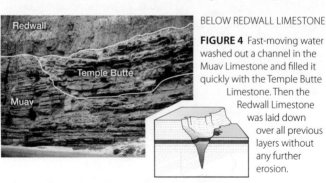

BELOW REDWALL LIMESTONE

FIGURE 4 Fast-moving water washed out a channel in the Muav Limestone and filled it quickly with the Temple Butte Limestone. Then the Redwall Limestone was laid down over all previous layers without any further erosion.

Below the Hermit Formation

Another boundary at Grand Canyon—the boundary between the Hermit Formation and the Esplanade Sandstone—is often cited as evidence of erosion that occurred over millions of years after sediments had stopped building up.[8]

There is a problem, however. The evidence indicates that water was still depositing material, even as erosion occurred. In places the Hermit Formation's silty shales are intermingled (intertongued) with the Esplanade Sandstone (Figure 5), indicating that a continuous flow of water carried both silty mud and quartz sand into place. Thus there were no millions of years between these sedimentary layers.[9]

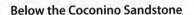

BELOW THE HERMIT FORMATION

FIGURE 5 Thin alternating beds of sandstone and shale indicate that the bottom layer (Esplanade Sandstone) was still being laid down when the top layer (Hermit Shale) began to be laid on top of it.

Below the Coconino Sandstone

Finally, the boundary between the Coconino Sandstone and the Hermit Formation is flat, featureless, and knife-edged from one end of Grand Canyon to the other. There is absolutely no evidence of any erosion on the Hermit Formation before the Coconino Sandstone was deposited. That alone is amazing.

Yet somehow a whole extra layer of sediment was dumped on top of the Hermit Formation before the Coconino Sandstone, without time for erosion. In places in central and eastern Arizona, almost 2,000 feet (610 m) of sandstone, shale, and limestone (the Schnebly Hill Formation) sits on top of the Hermit Formation,

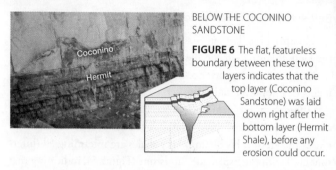

BELOW THE COCONINO SANDSTONE

FIGURE 6 The flat, featureless boundary between these two layers indicates that the top layer (Coconino Sandstone) was laid down right after the bottom layer (Hermit Shale), before any erosion could occur.

supposedly representing millions of years of deposition before the Coconino Sandstone was deposited on top of them.[10]

But where is the evidence of the supposed millions of years of erosion at this boundary in Grand Canyon area while this deposition was occurring elsewhere (Figure 6)? There is none! So there were no millions of years between the Coconino Sandstone and Hermit Formation, just continuous deposition.

Conclusion

The fossil-bearing portion of the geologic record consists of tens of thousands of feet of sedimentary layers, of which about 4,500 feet (1,372 m) are exposed in the walls of Grand Canyon. If this enormous thickness of sediments was deposited over 500 or more million years, as conventionally believed, then some boundaries between layers should show evidence of millions of years of slow erosion, when deposition was not occurring, just as erosion is occurring on some land surfaces today.

On the other hand, if this enormous thickness of sediments was all deposited in just over a year during the Genesis Flood, then the boundaries between the layers should show evidence of continuous rapid deposition, with only occasional rapid erosion or no erosion at all. And that's exactly what we find, as illustrated by strata boundaries in Grand Canyon.

The biblical account of the Flood describes the waters sweeping over the continents to cover the whole earth. The waters flowing right around the earth would have catastrophically eroded sediments from some locations, transported them long distances, and then rapidly deposited them. Because the waters flowed "continually" (the word used in the Scriptures), erosion, transport, and deposition of sediments would have been continually rapid.

Thus billions of dead plants and animals were rapidly buried and fossilized in sediment layers that rapidly accumulated, with only rapid or no erosion at their boundaries because they were deposited just hours, days, or weeks apart. So the evidence declares that the Genesis Flood actually happened, being a major event in the earth's history, just as God has told us in His eyewitness account.

1. S.A. Austin, ed., *Grand Canyon: Monument to Catastrophe* (Santee, CA: Institute for Creation Research, 1994), pp. 42–52.

2. N.E.A. Hinds, "Ep-Archean and Ep-Algonkian Intervals in Western North America," *Pre-Cambrian Geology* 463, vol. 1,1935.

3. A.V. Chadwick, "Megabreccias: Evidence for Catastrophism," *Origins* 5 (1978): 39–46.

4. In more technical terms, these two formations appear to intertongue, so the boundary is gradational. A.A Snelling, "The Case of the 'Missing' Geologic Time," *Creation Ex Nihilo* 14.3 (1992): 30–35.

5. L.T. Middleton and D.K. Elliott, "Tonto Group," in S.S. Beus and M. Morales, eds., *Grand Canyon Geology, 2nd ed.* (New York: Oxford University Press, 2003), pp. 90–106.

6. S.S. Beus, "Temple Butte Formation," in S.S. Beus and M. Morales, eds., *Grand Canyon Geology, 2nd ed.* (New York: Oxford University Press, 2003), pp. 107–114.

7. S.S. Beus, "Redwall Limestone and Surprise Canyon Formation," in S.S. Beus and M. Morales, eds., *Grand Canyon Geology, 2nd ed.* (New York: Oxford University Press, 2003), pp. 115–135.

8. L.F. Noble, "A Section of Paleozoic Formations of the Grand Canyon at the Bass Trail," *U.S. Geological Survey Professional Paper* 131-B (1923): 63–64.

9. E.D. McKee, "The Supai Group of Grand Canyon," *U. S. Geological Survey Professional Paper 1173* (1982): 169–202; R.C. Blakey, "Stratigraphy and Geologic History of Pennsylvanian and Permian Rocks, Mogollon Rim Region, Central Arizona and Vicinity," *Geological Society of America Bulletin 102* (1990): 1189–1217; R.C. Blakey, "Supai Group and Hermit Formation," in S.S. Beus and M. Morales, eds., *Grand Canyon Geology, 2nd ed.* (New York: Oxford University Press, 2003), pp. 136–162.

10. Ref. 9.

Geologic Evidences for the Genesis Flood, Part 7:

Rock Layers Folded Not Fractured

by Andrew A. Snelling

*I*f the global Flood, as described in Genesis 7 and 8, really occurred, what evidence would we expect to find? Wouldn't we expect to find rock layers all over the earth that are filled with billions of dead animals and plants that were rapidly buried and fossilized in sand, mud, and lime? Yes, and that's exactly what we find.

The fossil-bearing geologic record consists of tens of thousands of feet of sedimentary layers, though not all these layers are found everywhere around the globe, and their thickness varies from place to place. At most locations only a small portion is available to view, such as about 4,500 feet (1371 m) of strata in the walls of Grand Canyon.

Uniformitarian (long-age) geologists believe that these sedimentary layers were deposited and deformed over the past 500 million years. If it really did take millions of years, then individual sediment layers would have been deposited slowly and the sequences would have been laid down sporadically. In contrast, if the global cataclysmic Genesis Flood deposited all these strata in a little more than a year, then the individual layers would have been deposited in rapid succession, one on top of the other.

Do we see evidence in the walls of Grand Canyon that the sedimentary layers were all laid down in quick succession? Yes, absolutely!

The previous chapter documented the lack of evidence for slow and gradual erosion at the boundaries between the sediment layers. This chapter explores evidence that the entire sequence of sedimentary strata was still soft during subsequent folding, and the strata experienced only limited fracturing. These rock layers should have broken and shattered during the folding, unless the sediment was still relatively soft and pliable.

Solid rock breaks when bent

When solid, hard rock is bent (or folded) it invariably fractures and breaks because it is brittle (Figure 1).[1] Rock will bend only if it is still soft and pliable—"plastic" like modeling clay or children's play dough. If such modeling clay is allowed to dry out, it is no longer pliable but hard and brittle, so any attempt to bend it will cause it to break and shatter.

When water deposits sediments in a layer, some water is left behind, trapped between the sediment grains. Clay particles may also be among the sediment grains. As other sedimentary layers are laid on top of the deposits, the pressure squeezes the sedimentary particles closer together and forces out much of the water. The earth's internal heat may also remove water from the sediment. As the sediment layer dries out, the chemicals that were in the water and between the clay particles convert into a natural cement. This

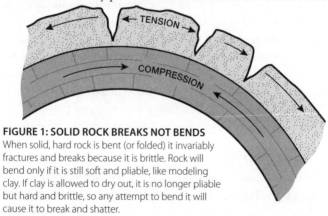

FIGURE 1: SOLID ROCK BREAKS NOT BENDS
When solid, hard rock is bent (or folded) it invariably fractures and breaks because it is brittle. Rock will bend only if it is still soft and pliable, like modeling clay. If clay is allowed to dry out, it is no longer pliable but hard and brittle, so any attempt to bend it will cause it to break and shatter.

cement transforms the originally soft and wet sediment layer into a hard, brittle rock layer.

This process, known technically as diagenesis, can be exceedingly rapid.[2] It is known to occur within hours but generally takes days or months, depending on the prevailing conditions. It doesn't take millions of years, even under today's slow-and-gradual geologic conditions.

Folding a whole strata sequence without fracturing

The 4,500-foot sequence of sedimentary layers in the walls of Grand Canyon stands well above today's sea level. Earth movements in the past pushed up this sedimentary sequence to form the Kaibab Plateau. However, the eastern portion of the sequence (in the eastern Grand Canyon and Marble Canyon areas in northern Arizona) was not pushed up as much and is about 2,500 feet (762 m) lower than the height of the Kaibab Plateau. The boundary between the Kaibab Plateau and the less uplifted eastern canyons is marked by a large step-like fold, called the East Kaibab Monocline (Figure 2).

It's possible to see these folded sedimentary layers in several side canyons. For example, the folded Tapeats Sandstone can be

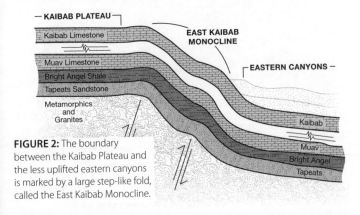

FIGURE 2: The boundary between the Kaibab Plateau and the less uplifted eastern canyons is marked by a large step-like fold, called the East Kaibab Monocline.

seen in Carbon Canyon (Figure 3). Notice that these sandstone layers were bent 90° (a right angle), yet the rock was not fractured or broken at the hinge of the fold. Similarly, the folded Muav and Redwall Limestone layers can be seen along nearby Kwagunt Creek (Figure 4). The folding of these limestones did not cause them to fracture and break, either, as would be expected with ancient brittle rocks. The obvious conclusion is that these sandstone and limestone layers were all folded and bent while the sediments were still soft and pliable, very soon after they were deposited.

Herein lies an insurmountable dilemma for uniformitarian geologists. They maintain that the Tapeats Sandstone and

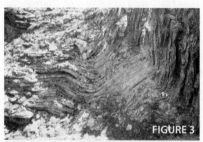

FIGURE 3

FIGURE 4

Muav Limestone were deposited 500–520 million years ago[3]; the Redwall Limestone, 330–340 million years ago[4]; then the Kaibab Limestone at the top of the sequence (Figure 2), 260 million years ago.[5] Lastly, the Kaibab Plateau was uplifted (about 60 million years ago), causing the folding.[6] That's a time span of about 440 million years between the first deposit and the folding. How could the Tapeats Sandstone and Muav Limestone still be soft and pliable, as

FIGURES 3 AND 4: It is possible to see these folded sedimentary layers in several side canyons. All these layers had to be soft and pliable at the same time in order for these layers to be folded without fracturing. The folded Tapeats Sandstone can be seen in Carbon Canyon (top) and the folded Mauv and Redwall Limestone layers can be seen along Kwagunt Creek (bottom).

though they had just been deposited? Wouldn't they fracture and shatter if folded 440 million years after deposition?

The conventional explanation is that under the pressure and heat of burial, the hardened sandstone and limestone layers were bent so slowly they behaved as though they were plastic and thus did not break.[7] However, pressure and heat would have caused detectable changes in the minerals of these rocks, tell-tale signs of metamorphism.[8] But such metamorphic minerals or recrystallization due to such plastic behavior[9] is not observed in these rocks. The sandstone and limestone in the folds are identical to sedimentary layers elsewhere.

The only logical conclusion is that the 440-million-year delay between deposition and folding never happened! Instead, the Tapeats-Kaibab strata sequence was laid down in rapid succession early during the year of the global cataclysmic Genesis Flood, followed by uplift of the Kaibab Plateau within the last months of the Flood. This alone explains the folding of the whole strata sequence without appreciable fracturing.

Conclusion

Uniformitarian geologists claim that tens of thousands of feet of fossiliferous sedimentary layers have been deposited over more than 500 million years. In contrast, the global cataclysmic Flood of Genesis 7–8 leads creation geologists to believe that most of these layers were deposited in just over one year. Thus during the Flood many different strata would have been laid down in rapid succession.

In the walls of Grand Canyon, we can see that the whole horizontal sedimentary strata sequence was folded without fracturing, supposedly 440 million years after the Tapeats Sandstone and Muav Limestone were deposited, and 200 million years after the Kaibab Limestone was deposited. The only way to explain how these sandstone and limestone beds could be folded, as though still pliable, is to conclude they were deposited during the Genesis Flood, just months before they were folded.

In this special geology series we have documented that, when we accept the Flood of Genesis 7–8 as an actual event in earth history, then we find that the geologic evidence is absolutely in harmony with the Word of God. As the ocean waters flooded over the continents, they must have buried plants and animals in rapid succession. These rapidly deposited sediment layers were spread across vast areas, preserving fossils of sea creatures in layers that are high above the current (receded) sea level. The sand and other sediments in these layers were transported long distances from their original sources. We know that many of these sedimentary strata were laid down in rapid succession because we don't find evidence of slow erosion between the strata.

As expected, the evidence in God's world totally agrees with what we read in God's Word. "Thy word is true from the beginning," the psalmist tells us (Psalm 119:160).

1. E.S. Hills, "Physics of Deformation," *Elements of Structural Geology* (London: Methuen & Co., 1970), pp. 77–103; G.H.Davis and S.J. Reynolds, "Kinematic Analysis," *Structural Geology of Rocks and Regions*, 2nd ed. (New York: John Wiley & Sons, 1996), pp. 38–97.

2. Z.L. Sujkowski, "Diagenesis," *Bulletin of the American Association of Petroleum Geologists* 42 (1958): 2694–2697; H. Blatt, *Sedimentary Petrology*, 2nd ed. (New York: W.H. Freeman andCompany, 1992) pp. 125–159.

3. L.T. Middleton and D.K. Elliott, "Tonto Group," in *Grand Canyon Geology*, 2nd ed., S. S. Beus and M. Morales, eds. (New York: Oxford University Press, 2003), pp. 90–106.

4. S.S. Beus, "Redwall Limestone and Surprise Canyon Formation," in *Grand Canyon Geology*, 2nd ed., S.S. Beus and M. Morales, eds. (New York: Oxford University Press, 2003), pp. 115–135.

5. R.L. Hopkins and K.L. Thompson, "Kaibab Formation," in *Grand Canyon Geology*, 2nd ed., S.S. Beus and M. Morales, eds. (New York: Oxford University Press, 2003), pp. 196–211.

6. P.W. Huntoon, "Post-Precambrian Tectonism in the Grand Canyon Region," in *Grand Canyon Geology*, 2nd ed., S.S. Beus and M. Morales, eds. (New York: Oxford University Press, 2003), pp. 222–259.

7. E.S. Hills, "Environment, Time and Material," *Elements of Structural Geology* (London: Methuen & Co., 1970), pp. 104–139; G.H. Davis and S.J. Reynolds, "Dynamic Analysis," *Structural Geology of Rocks and Regions*, 2nd ed. (New York: John Wiley & Sons, 1996), pp. 98–149.

8. R.H. Vernon, *Metamorphic Processes: Reactions and Microstructure Development* (London: George Allen & Unwin, 1976); K. Bucher and M. Frey, *Petrogenesis of Metamorphic Rocks*, 7th ed. (Berlin: Springer-Verlag, 2002).

9. Ref. 8; G.H. Davis and S.J. Reynolds, "Deformation Mechanisms and Microstructures," in *Structural Geology of Rocks and Regions*, 2nd ed., (New York: John Wiley & Sons, 1996).

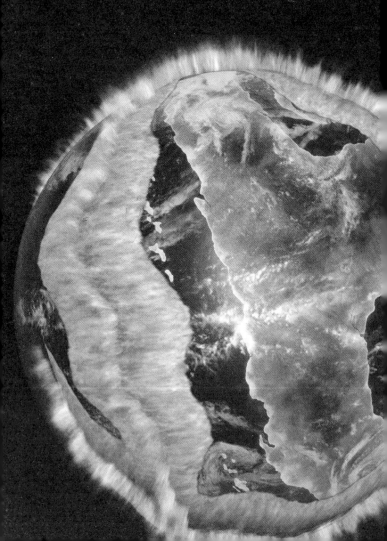

As hot mantle rock vaporizes huge volumes of ocean water, a linear column of supersonic steam jets shoot into the atmosphere. This moisture condenses in the atmosphere and then falls back to the earth as intense global rain.

A Scientific Look at Catastrophic Plate Tectonics

A Catastrophic Breakup

by Andrew A. Snelling

When you look at a globe, have you ever thought that the earth looks cracked? Or, maybe the continents have reminded you of a giant jigsaw puzzle, with the coastal lines of South America and Africa seeming to fit together almost perfectly. But what did this "puzzle" of land masses look like in the past? Was the earth one big continent long ago? What caused the continents to move to their present locations? How did the global Flood of Noah's day impact the continents?

Global investigations of the earth's crust reveal that it has been divided by geologic processes into a mosaic of rigid blocks called "plates." Observations indicate that these plates have moved large distances relative to one another in the past, and that they are still moving very slowly today. The word "tectonics" has to do with earth movements; so the study of the movements and interactions among these plates is called "plate tectonics." Because almost all the plate motions responsible for the earth's current configuration occurred in the past, plate tectonics is an interpretation or model of what geologists envisage happened to these plates through earth's history (Figure 1).

Slow-and-gradual or catastrophic?

Most geologists believe that the movement of the earth's plates has been slow and gradual over eons of time. If today's measured rates of plate drift—about 5–6 inches (12–15 cm) per year—are

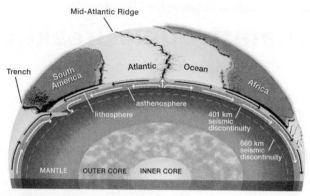

FIGURE 1: Cross-sectional view of the earth

The general principles of plate tectonics theory may be stated as follows: deformation occurs at the edges of the plates by three types of horizontal motion—extension (rifting or moving apart), transform faulting (horizontal shearing along a large fault line), and compression, mostly by subduction (one plate plunging beneath another).

extrapolated into the past, it would require about 100 million years for the Atlantic Ocean to form. This rate of drift is consistent with the estimated 4.8 mi³ (20 km³) of magma that currently rises each year to create new oceanic crust.[1]

On the other hand, many observations are incompatible with the idea of slow-and-gradual plate tectonics. Drilling into the magnetized rock of the mid-ocean ridges shows that a matching "zebra-striped" pattern of the surface rocks does not exist at depth, as Figure 2 implies.[2] Instead, magnetic polarity changes rapidly and erratically down the drill-holes. This is contrary to what would be expected with slow-and-gradual formation of the new oceanic crust accompanied by slow spreading rates. But it is just what is expected with extremely rapid formation of new oceanic crust and rapid magnetic reversals during the Flood.

FIGURE 2: Magnetic reversals

The magnetic pattern on the left side of the ridge matches the pattern on the right side of the ridge. Note there are "bands" of normally magnetized rock and "bands" of reversely magnetized rock. This sequence of illustrations shows how the matching pattern on each side of the mid-ocean ridge may have formed. In the Catastrophic Plate Tectonic model, the magnetic reversals would have occurred rapidly during the Flood.

Furthermore, slow-and-gradual subduction should have resulted in the sediments on the floors of the trenches being compressed, deformed, and faulted; yet the floors of the Peru-Chile and East Aleutian Trenches are covered with soft, flat-lying sediments devoid of compressional structures.[3] These observations are consistent with extremely rapid motion during the Flood, followed by slow plate velocities as the floodwaters retreated from the continents and filled the trenches with sediment.

A catastrophic model of plate tectonics (as proposed by creation scientists) easily overcomes the problems of the slow and gradual model (as proposed by most evolutionist scientists). In addition, the catastrophic model helps us understand what the "mechanism" of the Flood may have been.[4] A 3-D supercomputer model demonstrates that rapid plate movement is possible.[5] Even though this model was developed by a creation scientist, this supercomputer 3-D plate tectonics modeling technique is acknowledged as the world's best.[6]

Catastrophic plate tectonics

The catastrophic plate tectonics model of Austin *et al.* described in this chapter begins with a pre-Flood supercontinent surrounded by cold ocean-floor rocks that were denser (heavier) per unit volume than the warm mantle rock beneath.[7] To initiate motion, this model requires a sudden trigger large enough to "crack" the ocean floor adjacent to the supercontinent, so that zones of cold, heavy ocean-floor rock start sinking into the upper mantle.

In this model (Figures 3 and 4), as the ocean floor (in the areas of the ocean trenches) sinks into the mantle, it drags the rest of the ocean floor with it, in a conveyor-belt-like fashion. The sinking slabs of cold ocean floor produce stress in the surrounding hot mantle rock. These stresses, in turn, cause the rock to become hotter and more deformable, allowing ocean slabs to sink even faster. The ultimate result is a runaway process that causes the entire pre-Flood ocean floor to sink to the bottom of the mantle in a matter of a few weeks. As the slabs sink (at rates of feet-per-second) down to the mantle/core boundary, enormous amounts of energy are released.[8]

The rapidly sinking ocean-floor slabs cause large-scale convection currents, producing a circular flow throughout the mantle.

FIGURE 3: Model of catastrophic plate tectonics after 15 days

Snapshot of 3-D modeling solution after 15 days. The plot is an equal-area projection of a spherical mantle surface 40 mi. (65 km) below the earth's surface in which the gray scale denotes absolute temperature. Arrows denote velocities in the plane of the cross-section. The dark lines denote plate boundaries where continental crust is present or boundaries between continent and ocean where both exist on the same plate.

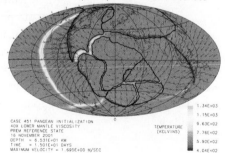

CASE 451 PANGEAN INITIALIZATION
40X LOWER MANTLE VISCOSITY
PREM REFERENCE STATE
16 NOVEMBER 2001
DEPTH = 6.531E+01 KM
TIME = 1.501E+01 DAYS
MAXIMUM VELOCITY = 1.695E+00 M/SEC

TEMPERATURE
(KELVINS)

1.34E+03
1.15E+03
9.63E+02
7.76E+02
5.90E+02
4.04E+02

FIGURE 4: Model of catastrophic plate tectonics after 25 days

Snapshot of the modeling solution after 25 days. For a detailed explanation of this calculation, see Dr. Baumgardner's paper, "The Physics behind the Flood" in *Proceedings of the Fifth International Conference on Creationism*, pp. 113-136, 2003.

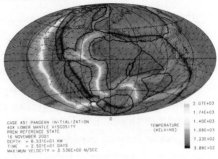

The hot mantle rock displaced by these subducting slabs wells up to the mid-ocean rift zones where it melts and forms new ocean floor. Here, the liquid rock vaporizes huge volumes of ocean water to produce a linear curtain of supersonic steam jets along the entire 43,500 mi (70,000 km) of the seafloor rift zones. Perhaps this is what is meant by the "fountains of the great deep" in Genesis 7:11. These supersonic steam jets capture large amounts of water as they "shoot" up through the ocean into the atmosphere. Water is catapulted high above the earth and then falls back to the surface as intense global rain, which is perhaps the source for the "floodgates of heaven" in Genesis 7:11.

As the ocean floor warms during this process, its rock expands, displacing sea water, forcing a dramatic rise in sea level. Ocean water would have swept up onto and over the continental land surfaces, carrying vast quantities of sediments and marine organisms with them to form the thick, fossiliferous sedimentary rock layers we now find blanketing large portions of today's continents. Rocks like this are magnificently exposed in Grand Canyon, for example. Slow-and-gradual plate tectonics simply cannot account for such thick, laterally extensive sequences of sedimentary strata containing marine fossils over such vast interior continental areas high above sea level.

Is catastrophic plate tectonics biblical?

The Bible does not directly mention continental drift or plate tectonics. However, if the continents were once joined together and are now apart, then the most likely time for their division was during the Flood. Some have suggested this continental division occurred after the Flood during the days of Peleg, when "the earth was divided" (Genesis 10:25). However, this Hebrew expression can also be translated to mean "lands being divided among peoples [nations]," which, according to the context, refers to the results of the Tower of Babel judgment.

Conclusion

Many creationist geologists now believe the catastrophic plate tectonics concept is very useful as the best explanation for how the Flood event occurred within the biblical framework for earth's history. This concept is still rather new, but its explanatory power makes it compelling. Additional work is underway to further refine and detail this geologic model for the Flood event, especially to show that it provides a better scientific explanation for the order and distribution of the fossils and strata globally than the failed slow-and-gradual belief.

1. J. Cann, "Subtle Minds and Mid-ocean Ridges," *Nature* 393 (1998): 625, 627.

2. J.M Hall and P.T. Robinson, "Deep Crustal Drilling in the North Atlantic Ocean," *Science* 204 (1979): 573–576.

3. D.W. Scholl, M.N. Christensen, R. Von Huene, and M.S. Marlow, "Peru-Chile Trench Sediments and Seafloor Spreading," *Geological Society of America Bulletin* 81(1970): 1339–1360; R. Von Huene, "Structure of the Continental Margin and Tectonism at the Eastern Aleutian Trench," *Geological Society of America Bulletin* 83 (1972): 3613–3626.

4. Steven A. Austin, John R. Baumgardner, D. Russ Humphreys, Andrew A. Snelling, Larry Vardiman, and Kurt P. Wise, "Catastrophic Plate Tectonics: A Global Flood Model of Earth History," in *Proceedings of the Third International Conference on Creationism*, ed. R.E. Walsh, (Pittsburgh: Creation Science Fellowship, 1994), pp. 609–621.

5. Papers by Dr. John Baumgardner in the *Proceedings of the First, Second, Third, and Fifth International Conferences on Creationism*, (Pittsburgh: Creation Science Fellowship).

6. J. Beard, "How a Supercontinent Went to Pieces," *New Scientist*, January 16, 1993, p. 19.

7. Ref. 5.

8. The key physics responsible for the runaway instability is the fact that mantle rocks weaken under stress, by factors of a billion or more, for the sorts of stress levels that can occur in a planet the size of the earth, a behavior verified by many laboratory experiments over the past forty years. See S.H. Kirby, "Rheology of the Lithosphere," *Reviews of Geophysics and Space Physics* 25 (1983): 1219–1244.

The Origin of Oil

by Andrew A. Snelling

For more than 100 years oil has been the "black gold" that has fueled transport vehicles and powered global economic growth and prosperity. So how does oil form, and what is its origin?

Basic oil geology

Oil deposits are usually found in sedimentary rocks. Such rocks formed as sand, silt, and clay grains were eroded from land surfaces and carried by moving water to be deposited in sediment layers. As these sediment layers dried, chemicals from the water formed natural cements to bind the sediment grains into hard rocks.

Pools of oil are found in underground traps where the host sedimentary rock layers have been folded and/or faulted. The host sedimentary or reservoir rock is still porous enough for the oil to accumulate in spaces between the sediment grains. The oil usually hasn't formed in the reservoir rock but has been generated in source rock and subsequently migrated through the sedimentary rock layers until trapped.

The origin and chemistry of oil

Most scientists agree that hydrocarbons (oil and natural gas) are of organic origin. A few, however, maintain that some natural gas could have formed deep within the earth, where heat melting the rocks may have generated it inorganically.[1] Nevertheless, the weight of evidence favors an organic origin, most petroleum coming from plants and perhaps also animals, which were buried and fossilized in sedimentary source rocks.[2] The petroleum was then chemically altered into crude oil and gas.

The chemistry of oil provides crucial clues as to its origin. Petroleum is a complex mixture of organic compounds. One such chemical in crude oils is called porphyrin:

> Petroleum porphyrins . . . have been identified in a sufficient number of sediments and crude oils to establish a wide distribution of the geochemical fossils.[3]
> They are also found in plants and animal blood.[4]

Porphyrins are organic molecules that are structurally very similar to both chlorophyll in plants and hemoglobin in animal blood. They are classified as tetrapyrrole compounds and often contain metals such as nickel and vanadium. Porphyrins are readily destroyed by oxidizing conditions (oxygen) and by heat. Thus geologists maintain that the porphyrins in crude oils are evidence of the petroleum source rocks having been deposited under reducing conditions:

> The origin of petroleum is within an anaerobic and reducing environment. The presence of porphyrins in some petroleums means that anaerobic conditions developed early in the life of such petroleums, for chlorophyll derivatives, such as porphyrins, are easily and rapidly oxidized and decomposed under aerobic conditions.[5]

The significance of oil chemistry

It is very significant that porphyrin molecules break apart rapidly in the presence of oxygen and heat.[6] Therefore, the fact that porphyrins are still present in crude oils today must mean that the petroleum source rocks and the plant (and animal) fossils in them had to have been kept from the presence of oxygen when they were deposited and buried. There are two ways this could have been achieved:

1. The sedimentary rocks were deposited under oxygen deficient (or reducing) conditions.[7]

2. The sedimentary rocks were deposited so rapidly that no oxygen could destroy the porphyrins in the plant and animal fossils.[8]

However, even where sedimentation is relatively rapid by today's standards, such as in river deltas in coastal zones, conditions are still oxidizing.[9] Thus, to preserve organic matter containing porphyrins requires its slower degradation in the absence of oxygen, such as in the Black Sea today.[10] But such environments are too rare to explain the presence of porphyrins in all the many petroleum deposits found around the world. The only consistent explanation is the catastrophic sedimentation that occurred during the worldwide Genesis Flood. Tons of vegetation and animals were violently uprooted and killed respectively, so that huge amounts of organic matter were buried so rapidly that the porphyrins in it were removed from the oxidizing agents which could have destroyed them.

The amounts of porphyrins found in crude oils vary from traces to 0.04% (or 400 parts per million).[11] Experiments have produced a concentration of 0.5% porphyrin (of the type found in crude oils) from plant material in just one day,[12] so it doesn't take millions of years to produce the small amounts of porphyrins found in crude oils. Indeed, a crude oil porphyrin can be made from plant chlorophyll in less than 12 hours. However, other experiments have shown that plant porphyrin breaks down in as little as three days when exposed to temperatures of only 410°F (210°C) for only 12 hours. Therefore, the petroleum source rocks and the crude oils generated from them can't have been deeply buried to such temperatures for millions of years.

The origin and rate of oil formation

Crude oils themselves do not take long to be generated from appropriate organic matter. Most petroleum geologists believe crude oils form mostly from plant material, such as diatoms (single-celled marine and freshwater photosynthetic organisms)[13] and beds of coal (huge fossilized masses of plant debris).[14] The latter is believed to be the source of most Australian crude oils and natural gas because coal beds are in the same sequences of sedimentary rock layers as the petroleum reservoir rocks.[15] Thus, for example, it has been demonstrated in the laboratory that moderate heating of the brown coals of the Gippsland Basin of Victoria, Australia, to simulate their rapid deeper burial, will generate crude oil and natural gas similar to that found in reservoir rocks offshore in only 2–5 days.[16]

However, because porphyrins are also found in animal blood, it is possible some crude oils may have been derived from the animals also buried and fossilized in many sedimentary rock layers. Indeed, animal slaughterhouse wastes are now routinely converted within two hours into high-quality oil and high-calcium powdered and potent liquid fertilizers, in a commercial thermal conversion process plant.[17]

Conclusion

All the available evidence points to a recent catastrophic origin for the world's vast oil deposits, from plant and other organic debris, consistent with the biblical account of earth history. Vast forests grew on land and water surfaces[18] in the pre-Flood world, and the oceans teemed with diatoms and other tiny photosynthetic organisms. Then during the global Flood cataclysm, the forests were uprooted and swept away. Huge masses of plant debris were rapidly buried in what thus became coal beds, and organic matter generally was dispersed throughout the many catastrophically deposited sedimentary rock layers. The coal beds and fossiliferous sediment layers became deeply buried as the Flood progressed. As a result, the temperatures in them increased sufficiently to rapidly generate crude oils and natural gas from the organic matter in them. These subsequently migrated until they were trapped in reservoir rocks and structures, thus accumulating to form today's oil and gas deposits.

1. T. Gold and S. Soter, "The Deep-earth Gas Hypothesis," *Scientific American* 242 no. 6 (1980): 154–161.

2. A.I. Levorsen, *Geology of Petroleum*, 2nd ed. (San Francisco: W.H. Freeman and Company, 1967), pp. 3–31.

3. B.P. Tissot and D.H. Welte, *Petroleum Formation and Occurrence*, 2nd ed. (Berlin: Springer-Verlag, 1984), p. 128.

4. D.R. McQueen, "The Chemistry of Oil—Explained by Flood Geology," *Impact* #155, Institute for Creation Research, Santee, CA, May 1986.

5. A.I. Levorsen, *Geology of Petroleum*, 2nd ed. (San Francisco: W.H. Freeman and Company, 1967), p. 502.

6. W.L. Russell, *Principles of Petroleum Geology*, 2nd ed. (New York: McGraw-Hill, 1960), p. 25.

7. Ref. 2, p. 502.

8. Ref. 4.

9. K.R. Walker et al., "A Model for Carbonate to Terrigenous Clastic Sequences," *Geological Society of America Bulletin* 94 (1983): 700–712.

10. Ref. 3, p. 12.

11. Ref. 3, p. 410.

12. R.K. Di Nello and C. K. Chang, "Isolation and Modification of Natural Porphyrins," in *The Porphyrins, Vol. 1: Structure and Synthesis*, Part A, ed. D. Dolphin (New York: Academic Press, 1978), p. 328.

13. J. Marinelli, "Power Plants—The Origin of Fossil Fuels," *Plants & Gardens News*, www.bbg.org/gar 2/pgn/2003su_fossilfuels.html.

14. Ref. 3.

15. R.B. Leslie, H. J. Evans, and C.L. Knight, *Economic Geology of Australia and Papua New Guinea—3. Petroleum, Monograph No. 7* (Melbourne: The Australasian Institute of Mining and Metallurgy, 1976).

16. A.A. Snelling, "The Recent Origin of Bass Strait Oil and Gas," *Creation*, April–June 1982, pp. 43–46; J.D. Brooks, and J.W. Smith, "The Diagenesis of Plant Lipids during the Formation of Coal, Petroleum and Natural Gas—II. Coalification and the Formation of Oil and Gas in the Gippsland Basin," *Geochimica et Cosmochimica Acta* 33 (1969): 1183–1194; M. Shibaoka, J.D. Saxby, and G.H. Taylor, "Hydrocarbon Generation in Gippsland Basin, Australia—Comparison With Cooper Basin, Australia," *American Association of Petroleum Geologists Bulletin* 62 no. 7 (1978): 1151–1158.

17. B. Lemley, "Anything Into Oil," *Discover*, April 2006, pp. 46–50.

18. K.P. Wise, "The Pre-Flood Floating Forest: A Study in Paleontological Pattern Recognition," in *Proceedings of the Fifth International Conference on Creationism*, ed. R.L. Ivey, Jr. (Pittsburgh: Creation Science Fellowship, 2003), pp. 371–381.

Should Fragile Shell Fossils be Common?

by John Whitmore

Have you ever walked along the beach collecting shells? Usually the best ones are thick and durable. Rarely do you find delicate shells in pristine condition.

In modern oceans, shells gradually dissolve in sea water or are consumed by other organisms. Experiments have shown that many shells, especially thin and fragile ones, disappear completely in a short period of time.

If the fossil record formed slowly, with individual rock layers taking hundreds or thousands of years to accumulate, you would expect fragile shell material to be relatively uncommon. Most of what we find should be thick and durable.

Creationists, on the other hand, would expect to find good preservation of all types of animals in the fossil record because we believe much of the record was made catastrophically during Noah's Flood.

Let's see what is actually found.

Studies in modern oceans

Taphonomy is the study of the process of decay and fossilization. Taphonomists have extensively studied the disintegration of shelly remains. They have run many experiments on crabs, snails, clams, and other animals with hard shells in modern underwater settings.[1, 2]

As expected, the soft tissue is usually gone within days. Surprisingly, the hard shelly material can also be destroyed soon afterward (days to years) by a number of processes, including the dissolving action of seawater, gnawing, boring, currents, and animals churning through the ocean mud in search of nutrients.[3, 4]

Problems and surprises

Rapid decay of hard shelly material in modern oceans has created a paradox for old-age, uniformitarian thinking. Taphonomist Thomas Olszewski is puzzled by the apparent discrepancy between modern studies and the fossil record:

This ornamented fossil clam had to be buried quickly in order for its delicate details to be preserved. In modern oceans, thin, fragile shells like this are destroyed quickly. Most shell material preserved in modern oceans is thick, because thin shell material can be quickly destroyed. However, new studies show the fossil record is not biased toward thick-shelled organisms. This is evidence that most of the fossil record formed catastrophically.

> Actualistic studies show that taphonomic destruction of the remains of shelly marine organisms can be completed on the order of days to years. Yet, radiometric and amino-acid age dating show that shells in settings where taphonomic destruction is ongoing can be 10s, 100s, or even 1000s of years old. In order to resolve this seeming

Mass accumulations of thin-shelled brachiopods are common in the fossil record. Even conventional geologists agree that deposits like this were made rapidly during storm events. It is common for thin shells in today's oceans to be completely destroyed by boring and encrusting organisms.

This fossil horn coral, found in the Flood deposits near Cincinnati, Ohio, had been bored and encrusted by various organisms prior to its burial. Organisms bore for food, nutrients, or domiciles. Encrusters, like the bryozoans (along the top edge of the coral), use the coral's hard surface as a foundation for their colony.

paradox, a number of authors have suggested that shells survive to great age by being sequestered temporarily from taphonomically destructive conditions and then reintroduced to the taphonomically active zone (that part of the sediment column in which a fossil can be modified or destroyed) by sedimentary mixing processes.[4]

Note the suggestion that shells must be "sequestered" from decay for many years in order to resolve the paradox between belief in old age and the observed rapid rate of shell disintegration. What Olszewski is proposing is that shell material must, upon death, be buried deep in ocean mud if it has any hope of preservation. This is the only way to protect the material from destruction.

The real paradox for the old-age uniformitarian is that ocean mud is not accumulating fast enough for preservation to occur; so why does the fossil record have shelly material at all, if it has taken long periods of time to accumulate?

An additional and more serious problem has surfaced for old-age uniformitarianism.[5] Even though small, fragile, thin-shelled animals disappear rapidly in modern settings, a recent study found that small, fragile, thin-shelled fossils are as likely to be present in the fossil record as large, durable, thick-shelled fossils.

Using the online Paleobiology Database (PBDB), scientists compared 150 of the most common genera of marine shellfish and snails (brachiopods, bivalves, and gastropods) with each other (450 total genera). The authors conclude:

Contrary to taphonomic expectation, common genera in the PBDB are as likely to be small, thin-shelled, ribbed, folded, or spiny. In fact, only six of the 30 tests we performed showed a statistically significant relationship between durability and occurrence frequency, and these six tests were equally divided in supporting or contradicting the taphonomic expectation.

The authors were surprised and confounded by the results because modern observations did not match their expectations. They concluded that the fossil record was not biased towards more durable shelly material.

One explanation that they did not consider, that would readily explain their results, is the catastrophic formation of much of the fossil record. The Flood would have indiscriminately buried both fragile and durable material together.

Conclusion

Creationists have correctly argued for a long time that preservation of soft body parts requires special conditions or even catastrophic processes. Now we can make the same argument for many of the hard parts found in the fossil record.

1. M.M.R Best, and S.M. Kidwell, "Bivalve Taphonomy in Tropical Mixed Siliciclastic-Carbonate Settings: Environmental Variation in Shell Condition," *Paleobiology* 26 no. 1(2000): 80–102.

2. S.M. Kidwell, M.M.R. Best, and D.S. Kaufman, "Taphonomic Trade-offs in Tropical Marine Death Assemblages: Differential Time Averaging, Shell Loss, and Probable Bias in Siliciclastic vs. Carbonate Facies," *Geology* 33 no. 9 (2005): 729–732.

3. S.M. Kidwell, and K.W. Flessa, "The Quality of the Fossil Record: Populations, Species, and Communities," *Annual Review of Ecology and Systematics* 26 (1995): 269–299.

4. T.D. Olszewski, "Modeling the Influence of Taphonomic Destruction, Reworking, and Burial on Time-averaging in Fossil Accumulations," *Palaios* 19 (2004): 39.

5. A.K. Behrensmeyer, et al., "Are the Most Durable Shelly Taxa Also the Most Common in the Marine Fossil Record?" *Paleobiology* 31 no. 4 (2005): 607.

Dr. John Whitmore received a BS in geology from Kent State University, a MS in geology from the Institute for Creation Research, and a PhD in Biology, Paleontology emphasis from Loma Linda University. Currently an Associate Professor of Geology, he is active in teaching and research at Cedarville University.

Dr. Whitmore serves on the board of Creation Research Science Education Foundation located in Columbus, Ohio and he is also a member of the Creation Research Society and the Geological Society of America. He has written various articles and coauthored an adventure book titled *The Great Alaskan Dinosaur Adventure*.

Flood Timeline

Date (AM)		Event
0		Creation
1056		Noah born
1536		God's proclamation of judgment upon the earth after 120 years (Genesis 6:3).
1556		Japheth born (Genesis 10:21)
1558		Shem born (Genesis 11:10)
???		Ham born (Genesis 9:24)
1536–86		God instructs Noah to build an Ark (Genesis 6:13–14). Construction of Ark begins. While we do not know the exact date when Noah was instructed to start building an Ark, it may have been at the same time as Noah started preaching in 1536.
1656		God instructs Noah to prepare to enter the Ark (Genesis 7:1).
	40 days	Noah enters Ark, and God shuts door (Genesis 7:16, 17). Intense rain falls 40 days and the fountains of the great deep open up (Genesis 7:11–12).
	110 days	Water covers the earth in the next 110 days and then starts to recede (Genesis 7:17, 24).
		Ark rests on the mountains of Ararat (Genesis 8:3–4).
	74 days	Tops of the mountains are seen (Genesis 8:5).
	40 days	After an additional 40 days, Noah sends a raven out of the Ark (Genesis 8:6–7).
	7 days	After another seven days, Noah sends a dove out of the Ark (Genesis 8:8–9).
	7 days	After another seven days, Noah sends out a dove for a second time (Genesis 8:10–11).
	7 days	A third dove is sent after seven more days (Genesis 8:12).
	29 days	Noah removes the covering of the Ark (Genesis 8:13).
1657	57 days	Noah and family leave the Ark (Genesis 8:14–16).
Total 371 days in Ark (360 in a year + 11 days)		

Rationale for calculations

Note: Years had twelve 30-day months to make 360 days. (See the preface in *The Annals of the World* by James Ussher.)

1. Months are given as ordinals; so subtract 1 from the number.

2. 2nd month, 17 day = $30 * 1 + 17$ = Day 47 of the year (Noah enters the Ark and the Flood begins.)

3. 7th month, 17 day = $30 * 6 + 17$ = Day 197 (150 days of the Flood) (40 days + 110) (After this, the Ark comes to rest on the mountains of Ararat.)

4. 10th month, 1 Day = $9 * 30 + 1$ = Day 271 (74 days later) (Tops of mountains seen.)

5. 11th month, 11 Day = $10 * 30 + 11$ = Day 311 (40 days later) (Raven sent out.)

6. 11th month, 18 Day = $10 * 30 + 18$ = Day 318 (7 days later) (Dove sent out.)

7. 11th month, 25 Day = $10 * 30 + 25$ = Day 325 (7 days later) (Dove sent out.)

8. 12th month, 2 Day = $11 * 30 + 2$ = Day 332 (7 days later) (Dove sent out and did not return.)

9. 1 day of new year = $360 + 1$ = Day 361 (from previous year, 29 days later) (Cover removed.)

10. Year + 1 month + 27 day = $360 + 30 + 27 + 1$ = Day 418 (57 days later) (Leave the Ark.)